MAKING
WILDFLOWER
MEADOWS

MAKING WILDFLOWER MEADOWS

PAM LEWIS

PHOTOGRAPHS BY
Steven Wooster

FRANCES LINCOLN

To my aunt and uncle: 'la fleur et la terre'

Frances Lincoln Limited
4 Torriano Mews
Torriano Avenue
London NW5 2RZ

MAKING WILDFLOWER MEADOWS
Copyright © Frances Lincoln Limited 2003
Text © copyright Pam Lewis 2003
Photographs © copyright 2003 Steven Wooster
Except pp 4, 6, 55, 61, 74, 89, 95, 113 (©
copyright Pam Lewis) and p 37 (© copyright
Peter Lewis)
Illustrations © copyright Ed Brooks 2003

First Frances Lincoln edition 2003

British Library Cataloguing-in-Publication data
A catalogue record for this book is available
from the British Library

ISBN 978-0-7112-2133-8

Conceived, edited and designed for
Frances Lincoln by
Berry & Co
47 Crewys Road
Child's Hill
London NW2 2AU

EDITOR Susan Berry
DESIGNER Anne Wilson
ILLUSTRATIONS Ed Brooks
INDEX Marie Lorimer

Printed in China by C & C Offset Pringting Co., Ltd

9 8 7 6 5 4 3

Contents

PREFACE

T HE ACREAGE of gardens in England is greater than the acreage of nature reserves. Thus we can play a significant part in saving our fauna and flora from eventual extermination. In this book, Pam Lewis has demonstrated one way of stemming the destruction due to modern methods of horticulture, agriculture, and unwise development. Furthermore, in the production of larger and more colourful garden plants, we have often sacrificed scent and nectar for colour and size. Let us retain these miraculous man-made garden creations, but also bring back the ethereal beauty of wildlife with fragrance and sweetness and the attendant song of birds – the tinkle of the titmouse and the heart-aching melody of the nightingale. A little strip of slender grasses can be sown with field flowers, while a patch of bare soil anywhere in the sun can become a miniature cornfield decorated with poppies, cornflowers, marigolds, corncockle and daisies.

Fortunately a few enterprising folk, like the author of this delightful and useful book, are willing to share their experience and the skills which can revive our countryside. Reconstucted habitats can save the dwindling birds, butterflies and bumblebees, and the perfume of hedgerows in flower. Moreover, who knows what undiscovered medicinal, life-saving or pain-relieving chemical is lurking in the leaves of some modest weed now threatened with disaster.

As Time tramples over us we tend to grow indifferent and chatter of the 'good old days', but fortunately wildflowers and the waving grass seed-heads of the hayfields, and the pools of bluebells under the beech trees, bring back the light-hearted past and a sense of forgotten wonder and happiness.

DAME MIRIAM ROTHSCHILD

A magical moment when, in autumn, the early morning light and dew combine to reveal the gossamer threads of silver cobwebs adorning the common knapweed.

INTRODUCTION

WHEN, IN OCTOBER 1986, we came to live in Dorset's beautiful, fertile Blackmore Vale, my husband, Peter, and I gazed reflectively upon our five acres of mismanaged, overgrown and soggy pasture, and began to understand why our property had been called 'Sticky Wicket'. Although there was a good 23cm (8in) of nutrient-rich, friable loam lying under the thatch of under-grazed grass, below that there was cold, unforgiving clay that would present us with challenging conditions and greatly influence our land management. Nevertheless, we tried to visualize how we would begin to transform our newly acquired property so that it would become productive and glamorous for us and also offer a flourishing haven for wildlife.

We decided that half our land would be planted and cultivated as part of our organically managed garden enterprise and half would remain as grassland pasture and hay meadows, connecting to both our small-holding and the garden edge. I wanted to blur the distinction between garden and holding, and blend them together to help the whole site melt unobtrusively into the surrounding farmland and countryside.

Step-by-step, we made three separate gardens to surround our house, which was set at the narrowest end of a wedge-shaped plot. The fourth – and wildest – of our gardens lies beyond and to the south, discreetly containing a large compound for our mixed domestic fowl and gently unfolding into meadowland.

Each garden has a special focus of ecological and seasonal interest, and colours are appropriately selected and arranged in a painterly way to support these intentions. Throughout the gardens there are several small grassland projects (described on pages 112-131). Our borders generously flow with both ornamental and native grasses, and with herbs and wildflowers grown among the garden shrubs and perennials, all helping to generate the naturalistic style that characterizes our garden.

The trick to making a wildlife garden is to try and mimic natural habitat, such as woodland, wetland and grassland. Hedgerows are also extremely important and in this respect we were very lucky: our property was already surrounded by 366m (400yd) of mixed species of mature native trees and shrubs. Apart from this, our plot was featureless, but this prolific boundary was a valuable asset on which to build and and provided a connection to the other varied habitats we would create.

To the north of the house, where the land lay at its lowest, we made a wildlife-friendly pond, with instantly gratifying results. Our first garden area was soon nicknamed the Frog Garden although, of course, the pond and bog also provide a habitat for a huge range of other creatures. I matched the planting colours to the predominant yellows of the native pond plants and celebrate the spring season with early-flowering bulbs and shrubs. I seized the opportunity to encourage dandelions, celandines and other wild plants to grow in the yellow-spangled flowering lawn.

Our kitchen window faces east and it was from this vantage point that I created a garden with special features to encourage birds to be our main wildlife guests. For this Bird Garden, I chose pink and plum colours for the particular range of plants I required in order to cater for the birds while composing a long season of sumptuous planting to set the 'ornithological stage' for our own delight! There is a horseshoe-shaped ribbon of grass which, of all our patches of turf, most closely resembles a fairly conventional lawn.

The Round Garden was designed and planted with bees, butterflies and other beneficial insects foremost in our minds. I selected a palate of flower colours that I arranged and blended to make a gentle progression from pale, pastel tints to the brighter hues of my nectar-rich ingredients. Flowering is timed to peak in August and last into September, when the greatest numbers of butterflies need sustenance and when bee and other insect populations have built up over the summer. My matrix of ornamental grasses helps to soften and integrate the plants in a way that is similar to the mix of native grasses with wildflowers in the meadows. On the perimeters of the Round Garden, we planted a small birch and pine woodland comprising just a dozen trees, a similarly small orchard and a belt of coppicing, which all help to provide token woodland habitat to support and shelter the various areas of grassland. These include a Chalk Bank and a gravel-based 'Mini-meadow', both of which are just a few metres (yards) square. On the Chalk Bank we can grow wildflowers which prefer well-drained soil and this, in turn, became the inspiration for the Chalk Mound in a corner of the Davey Meadow (see overleaf). All these projects provide sanctuary for displaced local wildflowers that we have rescued.

The White Garden – I call it my 'white wilderness' – could also be described as a fruit forest. It is full of plants bearing fruit, berries and hips, which we happily share

Plan of Sticky Wicket Gardens and Meadows
Our gardens and meadows have been designed to
offer maximum benefit to wildlife. The meadow areas
are numbered on the plan and an explanatory key is
shown opposite.

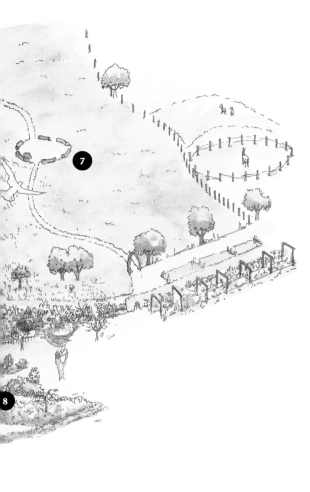

1 THE DAVEY MEADOW
One acre of lowland, fertile clay/loam pasture, typical of our area of Dorset; restored from horse-sick pasture to flower-rich meadow.

2 THE CHALK MOUND
Our most recent project designed to conserve a sample of our local downland flora.

3 THE WET, AND DRY, FLOWERING LAWNS (THE FROG GARDEN)
A sanctuary for those wildflowers which can survive well in grass that is mown for some of the year.

4 THE (ALMOST CONVENTIONAL) BIRD GARDEN LAWN
A wildlife-friendly lawn that is smart and easy to maintain.

5 THE CHALK BANK
The original chalk feature, which happened by chance, but turned out be a great wildlife attraction and the inspiration for the larger chalk mound (above).

6 THE GARDEN MEADOW
Our greatest challenge, where a mixture of wildflowers and naturalized garden plants grows in the fertile, loamy grassland within the garden.

7 THE NEW HAY MEADOW
An important conservation project where topsoil was removed to enable us to grow a diversity of wildflowers harvested from very few remaining local, traditional hay meadows.

8 THE MINI-MEADOW
A tiny patch of rescued turf growing – and seeding successfully – on hardcore and gravel.

with our resident and visiting birds and small mammals. Under this light tree and shrub canopy borders billow with native hair grass and purple moor grass, spiced with white-flowered ornamental and native nectar plants. Such grassy and relaxed plantings facilitate a smooth transition to our integral Garden Meadow, which forms the southerly fringe. In this L-shaped strip of land I grow a combination of wild flowers with garden plants and bulbs suitable for naturalizing in the grass.

Only a tumbledown stone wall and low bank separate the Garden Meadow from the New Hay Meadow, which lies immediately beyond. I custom-built the walls and banks to help provide extra homes and breeding places for the wealth of wildlife that has begun to inhabit the meadow. In 1997, our fertile, loamy topsoil was scraped away to reveal a clay-based subsoil which would provide suitable conditions for wildflowers – of local provenance – to thrive. A winding path snakes lazily through the concentration of flowers that bloom in a sequence that begins in April, peaks in June and continues more modestly until the end of September. A habitat-enhancing ring of logs encloses our 'pausing and picnicking spot' near the centre of this flowery paradise. It is my favourite part of our land and the point to which I am constantly drawn.

The Davey Meadow is separated from the garden by a quiet country lane and is of a more agricultural nature, having been grazed and managed as a small field in the years before we became its custodians. For a while it had been grazed solely by ponies and not managed so as to favour the survival of the wildflowers that had probably once proliferated. In this one-acre paddock we began the process of patiently restoring the population of wildflowers and associated wildlife. As former farmers, we well understood the necessity to return the land to a proper regime, comprising a combination of mixed grazing and an annual hay cut.

My own interest in meadows had begun during the 20 years I was actively involved with the management of grassland – on farmland, downland and horse pasture. During the last fifteen years I have been working on several meadows of a more domestic nature, in addition to my own. These meadow projects are connected to the wildlife initiatives I continue to set up and manage in other private gardens.

The information I offer in this book is distilled from extensive records I have kept of these and other very varied meadow projects with which I am involved. I hope it will help and encourage other landowners – especially gardeners – who have an interest in wildflowers and wildlife, and who may need guidance, as I certainly did at the outset. My own voyage of discovery was, and continues to be, extraordinarily fascinating but also long and convoluted. I found there was a wealth of technical information but a noticeable absence of practical written guidelines for the small land-owner/gardener/conservationist to follow.

Meadow restoration is by no means an exact science but, by understanding and following the principles of traditional meadow management, we can reinstate the correct seasonal pattern and put the grassland flora back on track. Comparatively little is understood or certain about 'meadow making'. The title is something of an anomaly because meadows, by their very nature, were not 'made' but rather evolved over hundreds, or sometimes thousands, of years. Nearly all of those original wildflower meadows have been destroyed and lost for ever. We now have to resort to emergency measures to try to shortcut the process of natural development if we wish to conserve the displaced wildflowers and their interdependent wildlife.

Meadow making is unequivocally not a substitute for conserving the few remaining flower-rich meadows that exist, but it is a vital addition to the ways in which we can help rescue a precious part of our fragile environment from further decline. There has not yet been a sufficient passage of time to evaluate fully all the implications of the creation of new grassland habitats but certainly there are some very promising signs.

Successful meadow owners can recapture the romance of a chapter in the history of our countryside, which has all but closed behind us. Some of us can recall the wonderful sounds and scents of the summer meadow; the clouds of butterflies, the collective drone of buzzing of bees and the distinctive ticking of grasshoppers. Surely not even all the perfumes of Arabia could eclipse the sweet, evocative scent of new-mown hay? In our own meadows, however small, we can take a nostalgic step back in time and pause in reverie of a more gentle bygone age.

So how to achieve a flowery Utopia? To see an enlightened way forward we first need to look back and understand the fundamental principles and practices, which led to the way meadows slowly evolved and then, quite suddenly, declined.

PAM LEWIS

HOW HAY MEADOWS EVOLVED

T
O GROW WILDFLOWERS one needs to understand the somewhat complicated interaction they have with their environment. Curiously, they seem to respond to hardship and trauma as part of their ability to find and sustain their place among their competitive bedfellows. Grass, scrub and, eventually, forestation are their adversary. Many grassland habitats are controlled and kept reasonably constant by some apparent trauma such as fierce, salty winds, extreme drought or even a fire or flood. Some grasslands are controlled by browsing wild animals, such as deer or rabbits, which also influence the proportion of competitive growth of scrub and grasses. In Britain, man is responsible for the way most of our grassland wildflowers evolved (and are controlled) by the manner in which he manages the meadows to farm and feed his stock.

Man-management

The term 'hay meadow' defines an area of grass that is cut for hay. Most British meadows exist because man originally cleared the forest and woodlands, and then managed the land for grazing or to produce forage for his beasts. (The word field comes from the old English word, 'feld', meaning a felled area). The wildflowers that typically grew in hay meadows did so because the system of management was consistent for many decades. While the grassland continued to be cut for hay and grazed (as long as it remained untouched by plough or chemical fertilizers and herbicides), it continued to evolve into ever-richer habitats where wildflowers and their associated wildlife could colonize. In fact, some documented ancient meadows are over 1,000 years old.

Grazing and cutting

A farmer would leave his grass to grow from March or April onwards. Then in June or July he would cut it for hay. Between July and March he would, at times, allow his stock to graze. During this grazing time the land would become 'poached' by the feet of farm animals, disturbing the soil and making some bare patches and ruts. Although this may appear damaging to the grassland, these conditions actually present ideal seeding opportunities for wildflower seed to germinate without immediate undue competition from grass and sometimes benefit from the microclimate of a small chasm. Wildflowers grow best in an open sward where grass is sparse and not too leafy or tall.

Soil type and fertility

The regular cutting and removing of an annual hay crop depleted the soil fertility of the grassland but the grazing animals would then return nutrients to the soil via their droppings. The equation balanced so that just sufficient fertility was provided for the production of successive hay crops. Fortunately, the nutrient content and level of this organic nourishment was minimal enough to favour the survival and development of a rich diversity of plants living in a brilliantly organized plant community. The smaller species would tend to flower in spring when the grass was short, although some later, shorter species would also thrive at the base of the more open areas of the grass sward. The age and condition of the turf held its own mysterious influences. There are recent, very revealing studies concerning the association between the soil fungi, bacteria and other micro-organisms which play a vital role in soil formation and in the inter-relationship with the plant root systems and resulting growth. Soil type and conditions (acid, alkaline, wet, dry, clay, sand, loam, stone, chalk and so forth) obviously affect the range of wildflowers that will grow. However, many are versatile and happy in a variety of conditions. (Sometimes plants will defy the predicted science and appear in unexpected places!). As a general rule, the most desirable wildflowers thrive best on impoverished soil.

Other influences

Weather conditions and even slight alterations to the management system – for example, whether the land was grazed by sheep, or by cattle or horses – might have favoured or disadvantaged certain plants in a particular year. Deer, rabbits and insect predators can affect the balance of plant species. The seasonally fluctuating populations of pollinating insects and the subsequent spread of seed from field to field by certain birds and mammals must also have contributed to the way the hay-meadow flora and its dependent fauna, evolved and varied within the season. The traditional hay-meadow system of management was constant and remained so long enough for a stable eco-system to evolve around the seasonal pattern that the hand of man imposed upon the landscape.

Causes of decline of hay meadows

There has been a sequence of events and developments in farming technology that have, over a period of time, conspired to alter the face of the countryside. Woodlands, hedgerows and wetlands have suffered untold damage and destruction and meadows, arguably, have suffered most of all. Here are some of the causes of lost meadowland:

GRASS CROPS

Sadly, with the land management changes that have occurred in the last 60 years, the system whereby the meadow flora evolved has been undermined. During this period, grass began to be grown in 'leys', which are regularly ploughed, sown with a single species of high-yielding, agricultural rye grass, overdosed with chemical fertilizer and herbicides, and then cut for silage in spring. Silage making became more popular as the weather patterns became less reliable and hay-making began to be considered too chancy a method of grass harvest.

THE CHEMICAL REVOLUTION

In the contest to increase returns from farmland, all broad-leaved plants began to be considered weeds and therefore the enemy of the grass crop. The application of herbicides, designed to target these broad-leaved 'weeds', also killed the wild-flowers; sadly, some of these were valuable wild herbs. Applying high-nitrogen chemical fertilizers to the few remaining fields of permanent pasture resulted in the more robust grasses and wildflowers gaining ascendancy over the more fragile ones. Compounding the problem, this loss contributed to the way the diet of modern grazing animal has, regrettably, become impoverished. The vital nutrients and natural medicinal properties of many of the herbs are no longer available in permanent pasture or grass crops, so farmers shot themselves in the foot by removing vital herbage on which the health of their stock depended. It is ironical that meadowland, after all this abuse, is then – in farming parlance – described as 'improved' grassland!

GOVERNMENT INCENTIVES

Acres of pasture were ploughed both during and after the Second World War to make way for food crops. Ecologically priceless grassland continued to be lost under the plough when government subsidies later tempted farmers to increase cereal crop acreages and to diversify into alternative crops, such as rape and flax. Once a meadow has been ploughed it loses the characteristics, developed over countless years, upon which so many species of plants and their interdependent wildlife rely.

THE IMPACT OF MACHINERY

As increasingly powerful tractors and machines were developed, hedgerows were destroyed so that fields were made bigger, and crops began to be rotated with ploughed grassland. Some weald and downland, hitherto regarded as unsuitable for agricultural development, began to be cultivated with heavy machinery designed for difficult terrain. Likewise, it became easier to drain and then cultivate wetlands (previously managed as water meadows), which were super-rich as a wildlife habitat. Later, as gardening became increasingly popular, so the market for peat became insatiable. These rapid and radical changes and demands conspired to further hasten the decline of meadows.

BUILDING DEVELOPMENTS

As road building spread a wide net over the countryside, and land was needed for house-building, quarrying and industry, very little account was taken of the way more and more of this irreplaceable grassland and wildlife habitat was being plundered. The cost to the environment certainly did not figure in the general economic evaluations.

THE URGENT NEED FOR MEADOW CONSERVATION

The devastation continued until we reach the point when, at the turn of this century, 98 per cent of our wildflower hay meadows have been destroyed in the last 60 years. As a result, a thousand years of evolution of this native grassland flora has been all but lost. The result has been devastating to the survival of many species of wildlife that the meadows supported. The fact that farming is now called the 'agro-industry' reflects the grasping and insensitive attitude to the way the land is managed. In the vast, sterile acreages of chemical-drenched crops, the scenario depicted in Rachel Carson's book, *Silent Spring*, has now arrived.

Recreating grassland habitat

It is tempting to think we can easily recreate species-rich hay meadows but this is not the case. As with antiques, copies or fakes may be attempted but the original can never be replaced. The first priority is to conserve the two per cent remaining species-rich meadows that are a unique part of our countryside and wildlife heritage. At the same time, however, new grassland habitat needs to be created as an emergency measure. From what I have learned, the only 'proven methods' for 'making' a meadow would seem to be to find some woodland with no trace of chemical residues, clear the trees and scrub, cultivate it, sow it with an appropriate mixture of seed from a local ancient meadow, allow it to grow and then manage it correctly, consistently, and without any chemicals whatsoever for an indefinite period of time. This is how meadows came about and, although hypothetically this would be a good formula for success, it might mean we would fail to see any results in our lifetime – even if we had some virgin land to work on or felt morally inclined to trade ancient woodland for new grassland! However, Dame Miriam Rothschild (who must surely be the patron saint of meadows) has shown us that a 'fair imitation' of a meadow can be made within 15 years. We need to start a new generation of meadows for the future generation of land custodians who, let us hope, will have the compassion, integrity and plain common-sense to nurture the land holistically.

The wildlife connection

There is a fascinating, complex and highly sophisticated inter-relationship between plants, fungi, mammals, insects, invertebrates and micro-organisms; alter or upset one part of the equation and you inevitably unbalance another. Nature has amazing powers of recovery but it is clear we have pushed the distortion to the limits. Will biotechnology turn out to be the last straw, I wonder? The pressure on our wildlife continues to increase, despite the raising of public awareness through the media. The plight of farmland birds is well documented, and seriously declining numbers of birds are a clear indication of the wider damage that is occurring through the natural food chain – a connection that, unfortunately, is not always fully appreciated. Loss of one species must have a direct bearing on the health or survival of others, be they plants or creatures.

Flora for fauna

The more I watch and learn, the more my fascination, respect and concern for nature grows. For instance, yellow rattle is a hay-meadow plant which is semi-parasitic on grasses and thereby helps to create and maintain an open grass sward where wildflowers and certain creatures can thrive. The nature of 'unimproved' grassland in turn affects the survival of meadow butterflies. They are very specific about the height, density and species of grasses required for their habitat. Changes in grassland management can have a profound effect on their ability to survive and proliferate. Natural predators can also have a direct bearing on the system. Countless colonies of species of blue butterfly were lost when myxomatosis was most prevalent in the 1950s. The rabbits died and, without their grazing activities, the grass grew long and so conditions were no longer conducive to survival of those butterflies that required a short, open grass habitat. Many orchids also grow best in open conditions and they are dependent on certain soil fungi, without which they cannot live. There are endless fascinating examples of these associations, about which expert botanists and entomologists are continually unearthing new facts.

Plight of displaced wildlife

I hope there will be time to discover more about nature and to conserve our British flora and fauna before the 'developing' world elbows out the last vestiges of natural habitat. Such wildlife as is able to adapt to an alternative habitat has so far been driven to seek asylum in parks, organic farms, gardens and the wildlife reserves that have been set aside for the protection of our native species of flora and fauna. Not all species can so easily adapt and many need very specific habitats. Some are severely threatened, some have been driven to the brink of extinction, some are extinct in the wild and some are totally extinct.

The looming GM cloud

The threatened growing of genetically modified crops will undoubtedly present an added burden to a healthy balance, and indeed the very survival of some of our plants and wildlife. Genetically modified, herbicide- or pesticide-resistant crops are designed to remove all weeds and certain insects upon which other creatures depend. None will slip through the net as has happened with conventional chemical weed and pest control. GM crop management will mean the perpetuation of the use of chemicals and an increasing dependency on ever-more toxic applications. No-one can tell us exactly what the knock-on effect of this distortion will be, or what other disruption might occur to alter the balance of nature. With the release of GMOs, not even our few remaining areas of wildlife habitat, nature reserves, gardens and so on will eventually escape contamination. Pollen and seed is not containable and will certainly spread – whatever blinkered politicians might believe. We will then have no yardstick against which even to measure the effect of genetic pollution. Fortunately the meadow story is not all doom and gloom. There is a growing public awareness and there are many new conservation projects are in place. Let's hope it is not 'too little, too late'.

Nature reserves and conservation groups
Fortunately there are charitable wildlife trusts and organizations concerned with conserving wildlife habitat, including grassland. Some valuable meadows are happily now owned and managed by people who understand and care. There are also encouraging new grassland initiatives in parks, in urban 'wasteland' and in schools.

Organic farmland
Farmers have to survive in business driven by the competitive market and the demands of the public. There are some welcome government-funded initiatives to encourage farmers to take wildlife conservation into consideration but I am not sure if the policies are likely to be sufficiently well-enforced or consistent for the necessary duration of meadow reinstatement. Fortunately, however, there is a huge rise in and interest in, and demand for, organic produce. The knock-on effect of chemical-free land management will produce huge benefits for the environment. Large tracts of grassland will inevitably be included. Prince Charles manages his Highgrove estate organically and shines a guiding light for both farmers and gardeners to follow.

The great garden network
There are waves of interest within the gardening world with some of our luminaries focusing on naturalistic planting and offering a refreshing alternative to the surge of quick-fix makeovers. There is a growing interest in creating small meadows in

gardens and this will undoubtedly help to conserve some of our native plants and the wildlife they support. Every little helps when we make our gardens wildlife-friendly. We may not be able to make perfect conditions for all the desirable and needy species to complete their life-cycle, but wildlife can benefit immensely from the 'corridor system', of which gardens can be a part. There are more than a million acres of gardens in Britain. This represents a vast potential space for plants and creatures to have permanent, or at least temporary, sanctuary as they move from place to place via hedgerows and road verges through urban areas as well as countryside and farmland.

Every little helps

I am lucky enough to have two paddock-sized meadows but I also have patches of meadow that are pocket-sized (just a few square metres/yards in one case). Small is beautiful too! The results are just as rewarding, but on an intimate and very manageable scale. I keep dreaming that if just 10 per cent of that vast acreage of gardens became patches of meadow grassland, we could reinstate 10,000 acres of butterfly and other wildlife habitat. Surely the time has come to take a rest from gravel, paving and decking and let at least part of our lawn grow naturally. We could do our wildflower and wildlife heritage and ourselves a huge favour and leave a more gracious and sustainable environment for the generation behind us.

MAKING MEADOWS

MEADOW RESTORATION

THE PRINCIPLES of this are the same, whatever the size of the land you may wish to have as a flower-rich meadow. You can adapt and apply this information whether managing several acres of paddock or converting part of a garden lawn. There is no point in trying to achieve the impossible. Wildflowers cannot be persuaded to grow in conditions that are not suitable. However, we can considerably increase the odds by improving, or even altering, those conditions to provide the best chance for the plants to thrive.

First look at your land carefully and make an assessment:

1 Can you identify the plants you already have?
2 What type of soil do you have?
3 What is the aspect of the site?
4 How has the land been treated in the past?
5 What wildflowers do you find growing in your nearby, local grassland?

I   PLANTS

Your existing plants will give a clue as to how close you are to achieving a desirable community of hay-meadow flowers. I suggest three (hypothetical) categories:

A If your grassland is composed of mostly fine native grasses and includes some desirable native plants, such as knapweed, bird's-foot trefoil, sorrel, betony, scabious, or even orchids. In this case, you are very fortunate and more than halfway there!

Ox-eye daisies epitomize our perception of summer meadows but they are a pioneering species, more often found in newly established grassland than in mature meadows, where only a few are likely to remain.

B If your grassland contains a mixture of native grasses (even if there are a few coarse ones) and of the more common survivors, such as dandelion, plantain, yarrow and meadow buttercup. In this case, there are hopeful signs. (Especially so if there are none, or few, of the more aggressive weeds in category C, below.)

C If your grassland has a large proportion of coarse grasses (including agricultural rye grasses). In this case, it is difficult to convert. If there is an added combination of aggressive weeds, such as docks, nettles, creeping buttercup, creeping thistle and agricultural clovers, the challenge maybe overwhelming. The more fragile species would never be able to compete with such 'thugs' growing strongly in this over-fertile environment.

2 SOIL

Loamy, alluvial or clay soil tends to be the most fertile and will favour coarse grasses and a small range of tall, vigorous species that we tend to consider weeds. Poor soil, on the other hand, will restrict the grass growth and encourage far more of the finer, more colourful wildflowers to compete. Chalky, stony or even sandy soils are better for wildflowers. The underlying rock – limestone, for instance – will affect the structure of the soil and its pH. Soil type, land levels and water-courses will dictate whether the land is well drained, damp, or even boggy. Results will greatly affect the way the land can be managed and the plant species that will thrive. Every meadow has a unique 'thumb-print'. We can select and introduce plant species in good faith but which ones will grow and survive is in the hands of 'Mother Nature'.

3 ASPECT

A sunny, open site is required for hay-meadow plants and most fields, by their very nature, have an open aspect. However, even on an open site, a north-facing slope will support a plant community that differs from the one which slopes to the south. There is an important area where meadow and hedgerow plants merge at field edges

The loamy, clay-based site of our New Hay Meadow has been transformed from a tricky category C grassland site to a buoyant category A meadow just a few years after the topsoil scrape and resowing.

and some meadow plants will tolerate a certain amount of partial shade. This is a useful point to bear in mind when making a garden meadow (possibly in an old orchard, for example).

4 HISTORY

It is helpful to know a little of the history of your land and what agricultural (or horticultural) 'improvements' it has undergone. Chemical fertilizers persist in the soil for upwards of 20 years (maybe 50 or more). Herbicides can leave chemical residues that can adversely affect the vital soil organisms that are part of the system of turf establishment. Sadly, there is no quick-fix solution to remove their effect: the damage is done. If your land has been kept free (or comparatively free) of chemicals, your chances of success are dramatically increased. Grassland that has remained uncut, while the weed seeds are left to proliferate, will bring an on-going legacy of problems or re-seeding. If the grass has been cut and the cuttings just left to rot, the fertility issue will have been compounded. Do you know when your land was last

ploughed or dug? Older turf will have a special ecological value and should be respected, even if there has been some degree of recent mismanagement.

5   LOCAL FLORA

If you are lucky enough to have a genuine wild flower meadow (or even an old, unharmed field edge or corner) near you, it is worth visiting to check out what is growing. Some churchyards are a good source of enlightenment. Local information will give you a good clue as to what you might include in your meadow mix.

Having made your assessment

If your grassland is category C, it may take many years to alter the condition and species content of the land. Your approach may need to be more radical - see Creating a New Meadow on pages 34-44.If your grassland is category A or B, then read on for advice about appropriate management.

The aims are to:

1   Reduce soil fertility.
2   Suppress the grasses.
3   Conserve the existing wildflowers.
4   Control/discourage the unwanted species.
5   Encourage a wider range of desirable species.

Meadow management programme

The following programme of management, 'The Meadow Calendar', is geared to reduce − or at least control the rise of − soil fertility so that ever more species of wildflowers can eventually flourish in a thin, short, open grass sward. If this programme of management can be guaranteed to be reasonably constant, year after year, your meadow should gradually become poorer in fertility and miraculously richer in wildflowers and associated wildlife.

Sticky Wicket is set in the bucolic surroundings of Thomas Hardy's 'Vale of the Little Dairies' in the parish of Buckland Newton. Our five-acre property had once been part of the common land known as 'Crane's Meadow' (but years of mismanagement had left the pasture devoid of the local flora which we have now reinstated.)

THE MEADOW CALENDAR

Spring

BE CERTAIN NOT TO APPLY CHEMICAL FERTILIZERS (EVER)

Organic manures, for example farmyard manure, are less harmful and persistent than chemicals but are best avoided. Beware! Watch out for incidental leaching of nutrients from fertilizer run-off from agricultural land, from nearby manure heaps or liquid run-off of effluent from silage, slurry or household cesspits.

❧

YOU MAY NEED TO ROLL AND/OR HARROW THE MEADOW

If the land has been grazed by stock, or is stony or rutted, it will need to be made even enough to ensure mowers will not be damaged. Harrowing will scarify and cure a build up of a 'thatch' of dead grass. If you are sowing any additional seeds, do so just before rolling. Seeds need to be in contact with the soil near the surface.

❧

ALLOW GRASS AND WILDFLOWERS TO GROW FROM MARCH ONWARDS BUT CONTROL UNWANTED WEED SPECIES

It is a good time to begin to control weed species such as docks and nettles. At the very least, prevent aggressive weeds from setting further generations of seed as they mature. Poisonous plants must be first eradicated where stock are to graze the land. (Some dangerous plants, such as ragwort and hemlock water dropwort, become even more toxic when cut for hay.)

Summer

This cut can be made between mid-June and the end of August. The earlier the cut, the more nutrients will be removed and the bigger the impact on the control of grass and some weed species, even if some of the flowers have to be sacrificed in the short term. If you leave some small patches of grass uncut, insects, such as grass-dependent meadow butterflies, are left with somewhere to breed; south-facing field edges (headlands) are ideal. You can alter the areas from year to year.

CUT THE GRASS DURING DRY WEATHER AT TRADITIONAL HAY-MAKING TIME

Large paddocks will need to be cut with agricultural machinery but for medium-sized areas (under half-an-acre), a motor-powered cutter (such as an Allen scythe) with scissor-action blades will be ideal. It will cut the grass in swathes, which are easy to pick up cleanly. These cutters are more wildlife-friendly than machines with rotary blades that chop the stems to bits and inevitably blitz a greater number of unfortunate creatures along with the crushed grass. Small areas can be cut with a strimmer but this can be perilous for wildlife.

CHOOSE AN APPROPRIATE MACHINE FOR THE SIZE OF THE PLOT

Leave the hay to dry so that some of the ripe wildflower seeds can be shed, and also to allow displaced wildlife to move away to safety. Your meadow is an ideal and desperately need habitat for wildlife, including an impressive range of insects. Hay cutting is unavoidably disruptive and can be lethal for some creatures. After the hay cut, surviving insects and insect larvae have a chance to crawl into the underlying turf. The denser the grass

LEAVE THE HAY TO DRY

sward, the more likely it is there will also be frogs and small mammals to consider, which you should try to avoid killing or injuring.

❧

REMOVE THE GRASS QUITE SWIFTLY

Remove the grass after about 3 to 7 days – it depends how you intend using or disposing of the cuttings. The length of time will depend on weather conditions and if the cut grass is to be made into hay or compost. Bear in mind: for compost-making, chopped up grass decomposes more quickly than long grass. Do not leave the cut grass lying around longer than necessary and be sure it is cleanly removed. Any decomposing debris may smother the desirable wildflowers and can eventually re-fertilize the land.

❧

ALLOW THE GRASS TO RECOVER

Allow the grass to recover for a few weeks. The grass then picks up momentum again and the re-growth is known as the 'aftermath'. When it has made strong green growth, further manoeuvres can then be made to debilitate it further. Each time it is cut or grazed, a little more of the soil fertility is removed and the chances of the survival and establishment of the wildflowers are thereby increased.

Autumn / Winter

IDEALLY GRAZE THE AFTERMATH (OR THE RE-GROWTH)

Sheep or cattle are better than horses. Goats are not efficient grazers. September to October grazing will have the best impact but stock can graze, at times, until the end of March. April grazing will delay and may reduce the impact of the flowering. Ideally, short, sharp, treatment is best, in other words high stocking rates/short spells – not always feasible to arrange!

༄

Alternatively, mow the grass aftermath in autumn and be certain to remove the cuttings. If the subsequent autumn re-growth is still very lush, it can be mown again in October or during March, or even early April. Bear in mind that spring mowing or grazing may be at the expense of the flowering of early species. It may only be necessary to target some particular areas if conditions vary and the grassland is patchy.

ALTERNATIVELY 'MECHANICALLY GRAZE' THE GRASS IN AUTUMN

༄

When grazing animals disturb (or 'poach') the soil with their feet, opportunities are made for seeds to germinate in the disturbed ground. Gardeners can simulate this activity, using any suitable implement that will scarify the turf. Additional seeds can then be added with an increased chance of their being able to compete. Seeds will be more likely to germinate from autumn rather than spring sowing. Including yellow rattle seed will help reduce the competition from grasses. Yellow rattle (*Rhinanthus minor*) is a pretty annual which is semi-parasitic on grasses and thereby suppresses their growth. The seed is only viable when sown fresh and it needs a period of cold to break its dormancy and enable it to germinate in spring. This plant is a great ally for the meadow-maker (see page 53). Wildflower plants can also be added in spring or autumn. Either plugs or plants can be set in, preferably ahead of a spell of wet weather. Where there are competitive grasses to contend with, larger plants of the more robust species will fare better.

AFTER CUTTING OR GRAZING, ADDITIONAL WILDFLOWER SEED CAN BE SOWN IN THE BARE PATCHES

CREATING A NEW MEADOW

I F, HAVING MADE YOUR ASSESSMENT, you find you have category C grassland, you can take either a pragmatic view of the existing situation or take courage and make radical changes. A fine line exists between plants that we perceive as 'weeds' and those which we treasure as 'wildflowers'. If it seems too daunting a task to try to persuade your meadow to alter its nature, you could try altering your attitude! As far as wildlife is concerned, rough areas of category C grassland are also extremely valuable for the survival of many creatures that may depend on coarse grasses and broad-leaved weeds.

If your heart is set on a category A meadow, then take a deep breath; to speed up the process of meadow making – by several decades – you may have to resort to extreme methods to reduce the fertility.

I can personally recommend the project I am about to describe but all the implications need to be carefully taken into account. Think hard, for instance, if you are considering disrupting turf that has been undisturbed for many years. It will have a very special eco-system of its own, and I must stress the fact that every effort should be made to restore rather than rip it up.

However, in 'no hope' situations, there are three options. The nutrient-rich topsoil needs to be either: 1 Exhausted; 2 Buried; or 3 Removed.

1 EXHAUSTION

Growing nutrient-devouring crops such as potatoes or maize is one method of ensuring exhaustion (provided no fertilizer is ever applied). However, it would be anybody's guess how many years it might take for the greedy crops to deplete the soil fertility sufficiently.

2 BURIAL

Either deep ploughing to bury the topsoil, or smothering the soil with a deep layer

Radical action is sometimes needed to make conditions favourable for wildflowers, some of which can be very choosy about their habitat. Meadowsweet colonizes the wettest parts of our meadows.

of an infertile substrate, such as brick rubble, chalk or crushed limestone will, in theory, bury the problem. Success will depend on several factors, particularly the depth at which the topsoil is buried and the nutrient analysis.

3   REMOVAL

A topsoil scrape removes the source of aggravation and may be the best option in some cases. We have had great success with our scrape, so I will outline the procedure we followed for our half-acre project. This involved removing several hundred tons of fertile, medium loam to expose a wildflower-friendly, clay subsoil.

The Topsoil Scrape

First considerations

You will need to discover if the nature of your soil is suitable. A soil analysis will reveal if the pH is acid, neutral or alkaline and if extremes have any bearing on the soil fertility. A mini-excavation will reveal what lies beneath the topsoil layer, whether it can be separated from the subsoil and successfully skimmed off to reveal it, and if that subsoil can then be lightly cultivated to make a reasonable tilth. A sandy subsoil is best. (We stripped away our neutral topsoil to a depth that coincided with a thin but convenient layer of gravel.)

Check for unseen hazards

There may be underground pipes or cables that need to be located and avoided. Mishaps can be expensive so it is wise to do a search if you are uncertain. (We discovered the remains of a very old drainage system that had long since become dysfunctional.)

Carefully evaluate the potential effect of altered land levels

Earth moving can profoundly alter the way water is held or drained away. The effect of removing the turf layer will affect the way water runs off or is maybe held in puddles. Neighbouring land and water-courses must be taken into account. In some cases, drainage systems may need to be installed or revised and sound professional advice may prove invaluable. The removal of our turf and topsoil altered the ground level to be a few centimetres (inches) lower than the part of the garden it adjoins.

We had unavoidably created a light 'sump' where water is sometimes held, particularly in one corner. With the turf removed, the rainwater was no longer temporarily held in suspension before gradually draining away and as a result the water flowed more rapidly over the surface and collected in lower spots. Although we made a virtue of having one area wetter (extended species diversity), we extended French drains into the existing land drainage system to relieve excess water from most of the site.

Some soil erosion may occur initially, especially on slopes
With no plants to hold the soil particles, soil is likely to be displaced in adverse weather conditions. For instance, this disruption could cause localized silty deposits or soil erosion and even landslip on steep slopes. The potential effect on neighbouring land should be measured, especially where the landfall is significant. The Sticky Wicket site just slopes slightly to the north. Heavy rain displaced some of the clay particles, resulting in a soil surface that varied between areas where loam had gathered, other parts with a pan of coagulated clay and some stony parts that drained more freely. We were fortunate that this did no great harm and, in fact, allowed a wider range of wildflowers to be established in the varying conditions.

Check the position of the scraped site in relation to nearby sources of nutrients
The scraped area can be garden sized – possibly a few square metres (yards) – but would need to be at least large enough, or on high enough ground, to prevent immediate and undue seepage of nutrients from surrounding or nearby fertile soil. At Sticky Wicket, we can now see the gradual effect from our mound of topsoil that, with hindsight, should have been sited further from the scrape. A hedgerow would have helped absorb some of the leached nutrients stored in the heaped soil. At least we made very sure our nearby compost and manure heaps drained in the opposite direction to our newly scraped site.

It may be wise to cut the grass short in advance of the landscaping
In this respect, the potential use of the spare topsoil must be evaluated in the short and long term. For example, leaving the grass uncut may have advantages if the

displaced grassy sods are to be used for building a grass bank. However, if the soil is to be transferred for immediate use in the vegetable garden or borders, the long grass would hamper cultivation procedures. I cannot condone the use of herbicides but creeping grasses, such as couch, will certainly need to be controlled. Making a temporary covered heap will eventually enable the grass turfs to become composted but there will be a rich store of weed seeds that may remain viable for some years. Our own soil seed-bank left us a lasting legacy of creeping buttercup and Yorkshire fog that together dominated the plant cover on our mount (see below). This highlighted the futility of attempting to grow fine grasses and wildflowers on rich topsoil. We knew we were on a hiding to nothing when we sowed the mount with an economy 'standard meadow mix', but we needed to prove the point!

Decide in advance what to do with the displaced topsoil
The quantity of topsoil will obviously depend on the depth removed and the overall size of the project. It may amount to hundreds of tonnes. The topsoil could be appropriately re-sited (such as for growing vegetables) or possibly sold – to help pay for the digger! Fertile topsoil may be the adversary of wildflowers, but it must be respected and valued for its complex, life-supporting properties. Not wishing to part with our own surplus soil, we turned it into a feature: a grassy 'mount' where our goats can graze and from which we can view the surrounding countryside.

Remember that dry weather is required for the excavations
Compaction and damage to soil structure and soil life can occur if the ground is wet. August is usually a good month for excavation, allowing time for soil preparation before sowing in September. It is advisable to make arrangements well in advance. It is not always possible to rely on contractors who are also at the mercy of the increasingly unreliable weather. (We just made it, by the skin of our teeth, before wet weather set in and lasted for months.)
Note: in some cases, planning permission may be required. It is wise to check.

With thorough planning and preparation, all we needed was a skilled and reliable local contractor, dry weather and closely cropped grass to make conditions ideal for the start of our half-acre scrape.

The   Landscape   Operation

For paddock-sized sites, hire a digger

There are diggers of all sizes that can be hired, with or without a digger-operator. There are even some neat little ones that can access the smallest of sites, leaving the minimum disturbance. When we tackled our half-acre site, we relied on the skill and judgement of our local contractor to provide the right machinery – in this case a large JCB – and do the job with the speed and efficiency that comes only with considerable experience!

For small, garden-sized sites, use a turf-cutter

Turf-cutting machines can be hired and are efficient in removing a layer of turf and topsoil to a depth of a few centimetres (an inch or two). You can then use the same machine to loosen the next soil layer or layers. The loose soil can be shovelled up leaving a few crumbs to make a seed bed. (I am not sure how well these machines work on very stony ground, but we found it very useful for small parts of our site which could not be accessed with the digger.)

Remove the topsoil to expose the infertile subsoil
In one stroke, this takes away the problems of the excess fertility, the coarse grasses, aggressive weeds and much of the weed seed-bank. A toothed (rather than flat-edged) digger bucket will help to leave conditions conducive for making a seed-bed and for seed sowing. Luckily, our digger driver was skilled and the machinery was appropriate for the job. An average of 18cm (7in) of topsoil was removed, leaving a well-scuffled surface in need of only minimal cultivation before sowing.

Tidy up after the digger if necessary
Pick up any remaining grassy sods, bits of root or large stones that may later damage the machinery used to maintain the meadow. In principle, reasonably sized stones are good for wildflower establishment. We trod in as many as we could and only picked up the very large or intrusive ones which could do damage.

Cultivate the ground to prepare a suitable seed-bed
The seeds need to germinate close to the surface, so the tilth does not need to be deep. Disc harrows, heavy harrows or a rotovator would probably be suitable for large areas. It will depend on the soil type and degree of consolidation after the digger. Small areas can be prepared with garden machinery or even by hand. We used hefty rakes and three strong chaps on our half-acre site and thereby avoided the extra soil compaction that can result from tractors with heavy implements.

Try to achieve a reasonably seed-friendly tilth
Consider whether to sow immediately or wait for the new tilth to settle. This will depend on the nature of the soil, the depth of the cultivations, the existing and impending weather conditions, and the time you have available before sowing is due. If the seed-bed is very fluffy (for instance after rotovation), allow time for the newly cultivated ground to settle. Be mindful of the fact the tiny seed must be sown, and remain, near the soil surface but that you need good soil-to-seed contact. On our sticky clay we sowed almost immediately, before it had time to become consolidated or compacted and in order to beat the advancing wet weather. To have waited would have been disastrous.

Calibrate the amount of seed required

Your seed supplier will guide you as to sowing rates, depending on your choice of commercially available wildflower mixes; err on the thin side – sparse is good. (See page 157 for seed sources). Sectioning off the land in strips will help to ensure a fair distribution of seed. It is highly advisable to mix the seed with an inert carrier, such as damp sand or sawdust. We used a generous quantity of the two combined carrier materials. As a rough guide, about 10g (⅓oz) of seed was added to a 14-litre (3-gallon) bucket of slightly dampened, 50:50 sand/sawdust mixture.

Use a seed drill or broadcast the seed by hand

The method depends on the size of your plot, the soil conditions and whether you trust your judgement with hand-sowing. The light-coloured sawdust will help to indicate the coverage and evenness of the spread of seed. A calm day is desirable; allowances for wind force and direction may otherwise need to be made. Obviously, do not be tempted to use even a grain of fertilizer! We hand-sowed, three of us walking side by side, about 5m (16ft) apart, rhythmically distributing the seed in a wide arc.

Roll to level the surface and create a good seed-to-soil contact

Either a flat roll or ring (Cambridge) roll would be suitable.

Note: do not be tempted to do this if the ground is wet. (Our sticky soil conditions made it impractical to roll, so on suitably dry days we lightly trod in our seed as we continued to deal with the odd large stones.)

Management in the formative years

The first year

If the fertility has been successfully reduced, there will be very little work in the first year. If the rattle germinates, the grasses will be held at bay and it is unlikely that you will need to cut the grass during the summer. This means you can sit back and enjoy the temporary cornfield annuals and allow the rattle to ripen and return seed to the soil to keep successive generations going. This will be an edifying year and somewhat untypical with regard to appearance and seasonal management. Results of germination can be unpredictable. Some seeds may remain dormant while some seedlings may be vulnerable to slug or fungal attack. The cornfield annuals and the yellow rattle should give a thin scattering of colour and pleasure but it is the developing perennial seedlings that are the main focus of importance. If, by ill fortune or mismanagement, the scrape was inadequate or if nutrients were inadvertently leached onto the soil, you may have problems with annual weeds and excess growth of grass. In this case, you will have to sacrifice the annuals and mow to control the situation. This is unlikely so I am assuming, from this point, that the scrape was adequate, as ours was.

Keep records to make the project even more worthwhile
It is worth marking out one or more 1m- (3ft-) square grids and keeping a note of the species that develop and change over the years. If site conditions are variable, additional grids may be sited to record noteworthy local variations. We use coppiced hazel stems to make a feature of two of our 25cm- (10in-) high grids. We also have a metal one that is more practical and enduring, and which looks quite discreet as soon as the grass begins to grow.

Create narrow mown paths for access to avoid disturbing young plants
This will avoid random trampling as you pass through the meadow to examine the flora and fauna. If you notice any patches where the ground shows traces of remaining fertility, steer the course of the paths in that direction to target the grass (remove clippings). We made very slender, snaking paths to facilitate access to each corner of the site and to the grids. We made a couple of stopping and passing places where we found odd patches where growth was livelier.

Look out for and control undesirable plant species
There will never be an easier time to deal with unwanted species. With the low fertility, problem weeds are minimized but remember: 'one year's seeding is seven years' weeding' and 'a stitch in time' and so on. In the early years, our weed problem was minimal and the few skinny docks that appeared were soon dug up.

Harvest and redistribute some of the seed as it ripens
To even up and increase the spread of the species, harvest the seeds as they ripen

and sow some immediately where needed. It is also a good idea to save a little for sowing later in autumn. Store them in a dry place in paper bags. We also sowed additional species harvested (with permission) from local meadows and from local lanes.

At the end of the season, trim the meadow to tidy up

The faded stems of the annuals need to be removed. There should be very little grass but, if there is, mowing is best carried out sooner rather than later in September, before the leaves start to die back. Always diligently remove any cuttings. We have now found an ideal piece of equipment for mowing small areas of meadow – a strimmer with a hedge-cutter attachment. It functions like a mini Allen scythe but is more easily manipulated to target some areas and perhaps leave others where late-flowering species are still making seed. Compared with a conventional strimmer, I believe this machine lessens the chance of injury to wildlife.

Sow seed or add plants of extra species

This is another good opportunity to sow or plant additional species, while competition from grasses and established plants is not too strong; the greater the diversity of wildflowers, the greater the range of wildlife that can be supported. It is advisable to try growing a few of the new introductions in pots for planting out when they are sufficiently robust. When we add pot-grown species, we seize the opportunity to remove any unwanted weed species or overwhelming grasses; the new introductions are put in their place – two jobs in one!

Management in subsequent years

Follow the same principles of traditional hay-meadow practice of cutting (and, if possible, grazing) as outlined in the Meadow Calendar on pages 28-31. Undertake an assessment of progress to make a suitable judgment as to timing the cut. The objectives are:

1 To keep grasses subdued.
2 To allow opportunities for increasing the diversity of wildflower species.
3 To take wildlife into consideration.

Assess the cutting time in terms of the grass growth
If the scrape has been successfully carried out, the grasses should not be a problem. The patchwork system of cutting allows you to meet varying situations on merit. If there do happen to be any coarse grassy areas, they can be cut in June or July to help reduce nutrients and depress the excess energy of the plants. Remember, it is vital to remove the grass cuttings.

Leave areas where wildflowers are flourishing until they have set seed
The seeds can be left to drop or be harvested for redistribution. It will also be helpful to wildlife if some patches are left uncut until after Christmas.

Vary the position of some of the grass paths
Wildflowers often find germination opportunities in the closer mown turf. In subsequent years, if the path grass is allowed to grow long, the new species are disclosed as they have their chance to flower.

Continue to introduce new species (by seed or by plant)
It is likely to be easier to do this in the formative years but there may also be some species that will need special soil conditions to develop before they will germinate and thrive. Soil fungi and bacteria, insects, and heaven-knows-what mysterious forces of nature may play a part in this. Wild plants need to be treated with great respect and the patient meadow-maker will almost certainly be continually amazed at the way nature's system works in her own time. Once the grassland eco-system settles into a pattern, there are increased opportunities for expanding the biodiversity. But, for most of us, it is easier to focus on growing an abundance of the desired wildflowers that show a willingness to thrive. Part of the fascination of meadow management is watching and recording the evolutionary process.

Mowing regimes will have a direct bearing on the establishment and development of the wildflowers. Mown paths often show interesting results but the debris should always be removed. They also facilitate a most inviting and practical access to other parts of the meadow.

TYPES OF MEADOW

I HAVE USED my own meadows at Sticky Wicket to illustrate certain practical points so far. This section gives further detail about each meadow and the surrounding issues of meadow management that apply in each case, along with information on some smaller meadow projects. The Davey Meadow is an example of meadow restoration and the New Hay Meadow is the one we have created from scratch. The Garden Meadow story describes the highs and lows of an on-going struggle to combine wildflower meadow-making with naturalizing garden plants in grass. The small and varied garden grassland projects tell their own unique tales. Each experience has fed me with information and inspiration to proceed with the other. Every meadow is a 'one-off' and the described management techniques and tools have to be understood and applied according to each individual set of conditions. This section tells the story of how we have approached the challenge in our own very different meadows.

My first goal was to create the sort of traditional hay meadows that my husband, Peter, and I used to manage in our farming days. In those heydays, meadows were 'ready-made' for us – a product of decades or even centuries of consistent management involving an annual hay cut and some winter grazing. In our farming years we had loved seeing the wildflowers, such as yarrow, plantain, wild red clover and knapweed, as we worked in the meadows, and we appreciated the herbal value of the plants in the nutritional and medicinal values to our stock. In spite of this, I must admit we rather took their presence for granted. Little did we realize that, across the country where farming was becoming increasingly intensive, chemical fertilizers

I believe it is unwise to underestimate the nutritional and medicinal value of grassland herbs, which have been all but eliminated from modern pasture. Plantain is one of the more likely survivors.

and herbicides were to be the death sentence for that diminishing number of meadows which had managed to survive being ploughed up and cultivated during and after the Second World War. I suppose we had watched it slowly happening but none of us could foresee that by now only two per cent of our species-rich meadows would remain. Rachael Carson and Dame Miriam Rothschild were 'on the case' but I fear they were lone voices. Now I hope I can add mine before it is too late, at least to help put some of our unique grassland flora in trust for future generations.

THE DAVEY MEADOW
(a restored meadow)

The site

Peter and I are fortunate to now own this mature meadow, which is approximately an acre in size (see pages 10-11). The soil is a naturally fertile loam on a clay base and the land is reasonably free draining in most places, in normal years. As far as we know, the grass pasture had not been abused with chemicals duringthe last twenty years but there have been periods when the necessary hay-meadow management has lapsed as the tenancy changed. We became the tenants in 1994, recognized the potential and began a programme of restoration, following the principles I have described in the Meadow Calendar on pages 28-31. From pasture that had become somewhat horse-sick and unmanaged, there has been a gradual transformation into a beautiful meadow where wildflowers and wildlife thrive in abundance. We have named it in honour of our dear neighbours, Roy and Jo Davey, who owned and loved the land for over 30 years.

The re-birth

At first, the number of species of wildflowers here was very restricted and included the less desirable nettles, thistles and docks that often arise where undiluted 'horsy-culture' has been practised over a period of years. However, after a few seasons of

The Davey Meadow, named after Roy and Jo Davey, the previous custodians of this meadowland. The paddock had been used solely for pony grazing for some time.

Peter's traditional hay-meadow management and, admittedly, some considerable 'species manipulation' from me, a brilliant transformation gradually came about. As an abundance of wildflowers began to proliferate, our acre of grassland attracted a wealth of wildlife and the original characterless 'paddock' was rekindled to become a dynamic 'flowery meadow' – as it probably once was some years ago. Wildflower seeds must have been in the soil seed-bank just waiting for conditions to be made favourable for the germination and survival of the plants. We just needed to hamper the growth of the coarser, less desirable species, take a regular annual hay crop at precisely the right moment and then graze or cut the aftermath of lush growth in the autumn.

Stock management

Our interest in making our land an attractive habitat for wildlife ran parallel with our interest in the holistic management of our stock. With the wellbeing of our horses and goats in mind, we needed to encourage plants with particular herbal value, such as dandelion, plantain and yarrow, that would enrich our pasture and hay with minerals and other essential elements. These plants would be equally valuable to wildlife so our two levels of conservation interest neatly crossed over. However, before we could even begin our programme of restoration, we needed to look at the wider picture and recognize how our land was set into its environment.

Environmental influences

What happens in this, and indeed in all meadows, cannot be viewed in isolation from the surroundings. The association with nearby features, such as mature trees, hedgerows, water-courses and roads, will affect the flora and fauna. Local habitats, such as woodland or wetland, may affect the range of visiting wildlife. There will be an impact from the way that neighbouring gardens or farmland is managed and whether public rights of way cross the land. Obviously, there are huge knock-on benefits where the adjoining land is organically managed. Wildlife road-kills and pollution from traffic emissions on nearby roads are an unavoidable disadvantage. Although we live in a delightfully rural area, the roads on two sides of our land are becoming increasingly busy. Nutrient pollution, known as eutrophication, results in plants being overdosed with nitrogen and phosphorus and we see certain plants gaining an advantage over others less able to deal with the surplus. For instance, nettles, hogweed and cow parsley prosper at the expense of most other species.

Hedgerow

A boundary hedge of mixed native trees and shrubs surrounds the Davey Meadow. The hedge is allowed to grow tall in some places (where ash and sycamore are dominant), restricted height-wise where power lines intrude, and annually trimmed in places where visual access is necessary for road users. Varying the way the hedge is managed allows the best possible range of habitat for wildlife. For instance, some of the meadow butterflies need a combination of both the open grassland and

hedgerow plants among which to feed and breed, and complete their life-cycle. Birds often favour the safety of the dense, trimmed hedge for nesting but rely more on the uncut stretches when roosting or foraging for insects and berries. Some butterflies lay eggs on the tips of native shrubs and can become victims of regular hedge control as the sides and tops are flailed. Both butterflies and birds rely on brambles as a most valuable and vital supply of food. For the butterflies to benefit from the very rich source of nectar, which contains three sorts of sugar, the brambles need to be in full sun during the middle part of the day. We vary our hedge management so

Native trees and shrubs in hedgerows provide protection, food and breeding places for many creatures, including certain meadow butterflies.

that one section is trimmed each year, some areas are left to grow tall, and, now and then, a section is cut and laid to thicken and rejuvenate it. All the thorny prunings are threaded back into, or laid on top of, the cut hedges. This reinforces the security of potential nesting places. A commemorative oak tree, grown from an acorn from a nearby tree, has been planted as a specimen near the north-east corner: a tribute to Roy and Jo Davey.

Field margins

The hedgerow plants that sketchily define the space where the boundary hedge now ends and the hay meadow begins are crucially important for wildlife. In traditional farming terms, the outer edge of the field is described as the 'headland'. If a generous margin of the headland is left uncut (or uncultivated if the field is arable), it becomes part of the 'field margin'. In more recent environmentalist's jargon, it would be redefined as the 'eco-tone': which is where one area of habitat blends into another. Call it what you will, this is one of the richest habitats for supporting a wide range of wildlife. Some of the meadow plants, such as dandelion, knapweed and yarrow, are equally at home in hedgerows. The field margins are good places to allow some of the coarser grasses to prosper in their own tangled way. For instance, cocksfoot and Yorkshire fog are not desirable in large numbers in the wildflower meadow but they are vital for the survival of some of the meadow butterflies, which lay their eggs on the stems. We leave a margin of about 2-3m (6-10ft) of this uncut, tussocky habitat, but we have to trim back the scrub growth where we want to prevent brambles or suckering blackthorn from advancing too far into the meadow. I love to stroll around the edge of the meadow and note the tracks, scrapes and holes that indicate the activity of field mice, voles, shrews and larger mammals. When at night I hear owls hooting, I feel assured that there will be a full larder for them in and around the meadows at Sticky Wicket.

Wetland habitat

The kingfisher is one of the rarely observed birds that can be found near unpolluted rivers. We have occasionally glimpsed the distinctive flashes of turquoise as we gaze down towards our western boundary, which is defined by the River Lydden. As the meadow slopes towards and tapers to this point, the land lies wet and extra fertile. This area was severely disturbed by mains drainage operations about five years ago and is struggling to settle back into an organized community of plants. Years ago, the flow of our river was controlled by a system of sluices that could be regulated to cause several of the local meadows to be flooded deliberately during the winter. The river silt would be distributed over the land, adding just enough natural fertility to ensure an adequate hay crop. In spring, when the land was 'shut up' for hay, the sluice gates were lifted and the water channelled back to the river, where it flowed on unrestricted during hay-making and the subsequent grazing period. There were some river edges that, because of the topography of the land, remained wet all year. This type of semi-wetland habitat is traditionally managed solely by grazing because hay-making would not be feasible on ground that it is damp right through the summer. So it is in our meadow corner. As a result, the species that abound here vary from those on the higher, drier grassland that is both cut and grazed annually.

A very hearty community of wildlife-friendly plants

In this damp, fertile area, the hay-meadow flora of our neutral, clay-based soil changes to include rather over-enthusiastic plants, some of which could, in other situations, be described as thugs and ruffians. However, they are all high-value for wildlife, offering pollen, nectar or larval food plants for insects and a brilliant seed source for birds. Most of the plants are beautiful and colourful though there are some who might question the aesthetic value of one or two. I have tolerated thistles, docks, nettles and the territory-grabbing great willow-herb, while encouraging or introducing hemp agrimony, comfrey, hogweed, common valerian, yellow flag, teasel, purple loosestrife, meadowsweet, figwort, wild angelica, and greater plantain. The latter tends to grow in or near recently made ruts or furrows but the remainder battle out the contest to gain domain in a wildly competitive floral community. Being the only biennials, the angelica and the teasel have to work harder for survival than their perennial bedfellows. The grasses include the tough cocksfoot, the dynamic tall fescue and Yorkshire fog, which is the bane of my life in other situations but just one more tough guy among this squad of bruisers! Greater pond sedge takes charge of the very wettest patches and both hard and soft rush have a strong hold in other damp places. Hemlock water dropwort grows close to the water's edge and I

cut this highly poisonous plant down and carefully dispose of it before it sets seed and spreads it into the water-course or onto any more of my land. I treat hoary ragwort with the same caution even though I have been told this particular species is untypical of related ragworts in that it is not harmful to stock. I can't afford to take a chance with my horses or put my neighbours' stock at risk. Scientists and experts are notorious for changing their minds so, as far as I am concerned, the jury is still out on this particular plant.

In praise of docks

I believe I may be among a tiny minority who find some docks quite attractive in certain situations! Docks are generally despised by both farmers and gardeners but they are good for wildlife, for instance seed-eating birds, and they support a considerable number of most fascinating beetles, including the dock leaf beetle. This metallic green chap feeds on the leaves and can reduce them to a lace-like skeleton. It can build up large colonies which have a considerable impact on the plant's ability to proliferate. This naturally occurring biological control procedure is being investigated and used by organic crop-growers. Without a doubt, sorrel, which belongs to the dock family, must be one of the most beautiful of meadow plants. On our higher ground, common sorrel grows and glows brilliantly, providing essential food for the small copper butterfly. The brilliance of the russet-red flowers is eclipsed only by the stunning colours of the visiting flocks of seed-feeding goldfinches.

Yellow rattle — a friend and ally

For centuries our surrounding Blackmore Vale has been dairy-farming country, where the fertile, gently undulating land produces lush grass in abundance. I have had to work hard to persuade the lusty vigour of this grass to abate. The regular removal of the grass crop has been the key to success but I have also had the pretty little annual yellow rattle (or hay rattle) on my side. I have one particular patch

Yellow rattle is a semi-parasitic plant with a preference for grasses. It draws nutrients from the host plant's roots and thereby restrains the growth. Once grasses are subdued, the wildflowers can flourish in a thinner grass sward without the overwhelming competition.

where the rattle is now abundant, the grass sward is correspondingly thin, and wild flowers are particularly prolific as a result. A 'natural' balance has been manipulated but it has taken some perseverance to nudge the system into operation. In the beginning I sowed rattle seed with disappointing results. I hadn't grasped the fact that although this plant is semi-parasitic and feeds off grasses, thereby inhibiting their growth, the rattle seedlings need sufficient space to germinate and develop in the first place. Just as with any other infant plant, it cannot easily gain a threshold where the grass sward is very dense. I did, however, have a little success from my attempts, saved seed from my small crop and persisted with rattle seed distribution in different parts of the field.

The rattle story

One year I noticed a thin ribbon of rattle growing in profusion along the length of a disused fox (or badger) track. It had found an ideal opportunity to germinate on the barer ground that had been carved out of a vigorous jungle of grass. I made use of this intelligence and, with a bountiful harvest of seed at hand, I set out to mimic the work of the fox. Bearing in mind that rattle seed is viable for only a few months, I started my campaign in late autumn when the lush aftermath obligingly mapped out places where the grass was most vigorous. Instead of choosing the greenest places, as I would previously have done, I set to work on the less fertile patches. I bullied the grasses and depressed the growth in the same way that the fox had done with the wear and tear of regular passage. During the winter I dug up some of the grasses and shuffled tracks here and there. As I progressed, I sowed most of the seed during autumn and early winter. In March we mowed a few more tracks and sowed the remaining seed. In April the seed miraculously began to germinate in the places we had targeted. The result was extraordinarily successful but we had to keep working on it for a few seasons before we could rely on its reappearance. From this nucleus 'rattle nursery', I have harvested dynasties of seed to spread not only across our own meadows but also in several other grassland projects.

The early-summer yellow haze of meadow buttercups is punctuated by glowing red sorrel and the silvery flowerheads of crested dog's-tail. The next flowering sequence of meadow crane's-bills and corky-fruited water dropwort is waiting in the wings.

Taking stock of, and appreciating, the existing wildflowers

As soon as the rattle began its work on grass control, it was easier to identify the type and proportion of wildflower species we had growing. There were no rare or extraordinary plants, although I count corky-fruited water dropwort as a very special guest, belonging as it does exclusively to south-west England. The plants in the Davey Meadow were exactly what might have been predicted for the locality and the conditions. After a welcome early scattering of dandelions intermingled with ribwort plantains and ladies' smock, the meadow becomes a yellow haze of meadow buttercups and rattle, interspersed by glowing flecks of russet-red sorrel. When I look closely at the base of the grass sward, I see that there is a scattering of lesser stitchwort permeating the lower regions in a sweetly understated way. I have introduced the meadow crane's-bills which flower with the corky-fruited water dropwort. Together with the ox-eye daisies, they change the fading buttercup-dominated scene from a yellow to a predominantly white canvas, just touched with

blue (of both crane's-bills and the less conspicuous selfheal). Purple knapweeds then permeate the whiteness and take over the show for several weeks, during which time they are joined by blue tufted vetch, the yellows of bird's-foot trefoil, meadow vetchling and cat's-ear, and the fluffy stems of creamy white meadowsweet. For the finale, there is a sprinkling of fine, lacy white heads of wild carrot and patches of flat white heads of yarrow.

Meadowsweet – friend or foe?

There is a shallow depression that crosses our meadow. Even this very slight difference in land levels causes an interesting alteration in water retention and therefore corresponding plant species. We find a notable seam of meadowsweet that is revealed as a white frothy band in July. It is richly fragrant and very beautiful but can be quite invasive. The root system is woody and dense, and other plants become effectively excluded from their impenetrable stronghold. At the end of May I mow a path around and, in places, through the densest patch. This reduces the aggravation and allows us to wander among the uncut, fluffy belt and sample the fragrance as we gather some of the flowerheads to dry for herbal uses. The remaining flower-heads are mown just before they set seed to prevent them advancing their territory.

Nutrient attack!

In another small area, the meadow flora is dramatically altered by the adverse effect of a combination of water and excess fertility, which seeps in from a neighbour's septic tank. This aggravates the spread of meadowsweet and also results in a patch of land where nettles dominate but share some space with the robust great willow-herb. I wish I had the courage to plant some reeds to absorb some of the impurities that must find their way into the nearby river, but I fear an uncontrollable spread of reed may invade my meadow and cause more problems than I could hope to resolve. I have, however, planted a small barrier of willows to help minimize the pollution. I can control the willows with regular coppicing. A mature boundary hedge also helps absorb some of the nutrients but, as a result, it grows with a vengeance and casts considerable shade. I am not convinced this nettle patch receives sufficient sunlight to be useful for breeding butterflies but maybe the hawk moths breed on the willow-herb, which is the host plant for its caterpillars.

Nettles need to be valued

Nettles are good indicators of patches of extra fertile soil and they are vital wildlife plants. They are the food plant of the larvae of the peacock, red admiral and small tortoiseshell butterflies and are occasionally used by painted lady and comma butterflies. The comma apparently sometimes breeds on nettles in more shaded hedgerows so maybe conditions are favourable for them in what I consider to be a bit of a problem area. Nettles also support specific early aphids that are an essential part of the spring diet of emerging ladybird larvae. Despite my pragmatic attitude towards my nettle sanctuary, I do wish to contain them and prevent an invasion. This meadow of mine is one of those rare phenomenon – wildflowers growing on land that is fertile but whose fertility has not been 'enhanced' by chemical fertilizers. Keeping the balance of fertility is the key to sustaining and increasing the diversity of species of our meadow flora. So far, the nettles miraculously confine themselves to the one place where excessive fertility – albeit organic – has unavoidably seeped in. If this was a south-facing spot, such as the one at the south-eastern end, I would cut the nettles before they made seed and add them to the compost heap, where their super-store of nitrogen would help break down the drier materials. The more palatable regrowth of nettles would then be just right for the later broods of butterflies. I try to remember to do this in the more appropriate, sunny parts of the hedgerow and have often been rewarded with families of dark, furry caterpillars. It is important to leave at least a small proportion of the maturing nettles uncut for the caterpillars to pupate on. In winter, the grazing stock will feed on the old stems and benefit from the nutritional and herbal attributes.

Confining aggressive species

It would be an uphill struggle to attempt to weaken the nettle stronghold but, as with the meadowsweet, I can at least prevent the vegetative spread by regularly mowing the perimeter of this patch. The same principle applies to creeping thistle that is a menace in grassland and is on the Department of Food and Agriculture's proscribed list. In spite of this, it is a wonderful nectar plant, the favoured food plant for the exquisite painted lady butterfly and, to my way of thinking, has one of the most evocative and sumptuous scents of the summer meadow. Despite its ill repute, I cannot dislike it although I certainly wish to confine the spread. Thistles in hay make bale handling notoriously painful; thistles spreading to neighbouring land can make one most unpopular! The 'cut-off' mowing strategy works provided the width of the cut-off band is adequate (creeping plants of this tenacity are hard to keep in bounds). My mown band is about 4-5m (13-16ft) at this point, and is regularly worn by cars entering the parking plot that runs along the southern boundary. Is the mowing band the controlling factor or does the wear and tear of traffic help? I don't know the answer but – so far – the thistles are held at bay.

Selected grasses

I was lucky that the Davey Meadow supported a wide range of native grasses, most of which were useful in respect of grazing and hay-making, and most of them an ideal 'mixer' for meadow flowers as well as a welcome habitat for resident wildlife, especially butterflies. Crested dog's-tail, sweet vernal, the fescues and both rough and smooth meadow grass were ideal, especially when the yellow rattle tapped into their root systems, pinched their nutrients and kept them subdued. Small Timothy was no bother and I was relieved that there were no oversized, bully-boy agricultural varieties. The similar-looking, earlier-flowering meadow foxtail tended to monopolize certain patches and few wildflowers grew among it. An extra application of rattle eventually evened things out, but I miss seeing the mass of dynamic, dancing flowerheads criss-crossing in the breeze above the early spring flowers and shorter grasses. Cocksfoot, another lovely grass but rather a hefty individual, was fortunately not too over-abundant and, miraculously, neither was the terrorizing Yorkshire fog. The latter spreads its soft floppy leaves, reminding me of a broody hen settling herself. By sheer volume, it can suffocate any nearby seedlings and elbow out neighbouring plants as it gets busy making another generation of itself by seed. True, the flowers are very beautiful but I can't forgive the way it has monopolized the grass species in parts of my other pasture. I took care to avoid spreading rattle close to the hedgerows where I wanted to uphold the tussocky character of all the coarser

Only the most robust wildflowers, such as corky-fruited water dropwort, can survive the competition from clumpy grasses such as Yorkshire fog, but, with a well-balanced grass mixture, others, such as sorrel, can take their place, look enchanting and help to support wildlife.

grasses, which were naturally confined to the field edges owing to the fact they were never cut and seldom grazed.

The 'patchwork' system for mowing

However, at the end of May we begin our mowing regime elsewhere. Apart from mowing (or grazing) our car-parking zone, we also mow narrow, winding paths along which we can wander and enjoy our wildflowers and wildlife. These paths are just a ride-on mower's width and have several purposes and extra advantages for wildlife, some of which rejoice in a variety of lengths of grass. After the minimum space for our garden visitors' car parking has been allocated, we mow these paths to divide the meadow into three sections, making a patchwork of grassy areas. Each year we can rotate the order of the eventual hay cuts and/or grazing regimes and target the section that has the most vigorous grass growth to receive the earliest cut. The plan is to consistently reduce the vigour of the grasses and to achieve a thin, airy, open grass sward. The cutting and grazing programme, combined with the establishment of yellow rattle, has worked miracles. I can easily tell where we have or have not succeeded in debilitating lusty growth. Where the vegetation is dense, passing animals, especially foxes, badgers and dogs, leave tracks and rather annoying, disenchantingly flattened patches but in other parts of the meadow, where the grass-to-wildflower status is reaching perfection, there is no evidence of trespass. For instance, my three whippets can race through these fine areas leaving no trace of disturbance in their wake. Hay-making in the Davey Meadow takes place, in three phases, between the end of June and the end of August. The patchwork system has proved very beneficial for the wellbeing of plants, wildlife – and whippets!

Grass cutting

We first had to resolve the problem of discovering and securing the right equipment for grass cutting and hay-making. It largely depends on the size of the

Hay-making at Sticky Wicket is a family activity, as it was for hundreds of years before farming became mechanized. Emma helps Peter stack the hay into old-fashioned hay-cocks on wooden tripods.

patch being cut. In the past, we used to hire an agricultural contractor to cut and bale our hay. However, it has become increasingly hard to persuade a busy contractor to be involved with tiny meadows, when both machinery and operators are geared to dealing with vast acreages of grass that, in most cases, are cut for silage about a month earlier. Hay-making has gone out of fashion, leaving those of us with meadows or pony paddocks up a creek, with no-one to help us paddle. We now use a ride-on mower (a Countax) for the early (May/June) cut that we carry out for parking and paths. It copes quite adequately with long grass as long as it is not too thick and tangled, as it can become later in the year. I would like to be able to recount how we cut the hay crop in the old-fashioned way, with a scythe, but so far, unfortunately, I have made a mockery of trying to master the skill. Instead, we follow the later farming tradition by using a vintage, tractor-mounted mower that has a twin multi-toothed cutter bar with reciprocating (scissor-action) blades. The cut grass is left in gentle, wave-like swathes that are easy either to pick up and remove while they are still green or that we can fluff up, allow to dry and harvest for hay.

Alternative methods

A viable alternative would be to hire a motor-powered Allen scythe that cuts in the same way. I believe these forms of cutting machinery, compared to the fiercer, whirring rotary blades, are less likely to cause injury and fatalities to wildlife. Allen scythes can be quite heavy, and rather 'self-willed' to operate in small spaces, on sloping ground, or where there are trees to avoid. For small patches of meadow, or isolated problem areas, we are experimenting with a strimmer with a hedge- or scrub-cutter bar that also cuts in a similar way. So far results seem to be very encouraging and this may prove to be a useful tool when dealing with small patches of 'garden meadow'. There are also wheeled strimmers with up to four plastic strings but I have not tried these machines because I fear the grass would be mashed in the process. Not so good for wildlife, hopeless for hay-making, but an option to consider if the grass is to be composted rather than being made into hay. Chopped-up grass decomposes much more efficiently than long grass, but I find it more tedious to rake up.

What to do with the grass?

Where possible we make hay to feed to our stock in winter. The earliest cut has the greatest nutrient value but even the late cut has the benefit of containing valuable, mineral-rich herbage that is sadly absent in modern grass crops. If the grass is spoiled by rain, we use some of it to mulch the newly planted native trees and shrubs that have been added to boost the diversity of the species in the hedgerow. The rest is composted along with the droppings, most of which we regularly pick up whenever the horses are put out to graze in the meadow. The fresh mowings from the paths add the extra nitrogenous ingredient to help the compost heap heat up and digest the stalky, carbon-rich hay, and the 'weed' seeds. The compost is then soon taken away and used to enrich the garden soil. One way or another, the nutrients from the soil in the Davey Meadow end up feeding the things that truly profit from this nourishment and meanwhile the level of the fertility in the meadow is lowered a little each year to the advantage of the wildflowers; a most satisfying arrangement but we are fortunate to be able to recycle the materials in this way. If this were not the case, I would investigate the possibility of persuading the council to take away the organic debris and use it as a valuable ingredient for their recycling department, which makes garden compost.

The extra benefits of 'patchworking'

There are four other distinct advantages to the strategy of 'patchwork' cutting. Firstly, tackling small sections at a time takes some of the pain and strain out of the physically taxing (though pleasurable) effort of hay-making by hand. The strain comes from trying to dodge the increasingly unpredictable weather, so, secondly, the three-stage hay-cutting allows us a fighting chance of catching at least one spell of warm, dry weather in which to stook our small hay crop onto our specially constructed wooden tripods. Our wildlife receives the third benefit; hay-making is unfortunately not without casualties to some of the grassland-dependent creatures. However, by 'patchworking' not all the damage will occur in one fell swoop and at least some survivors will creep or crawl to the safety of the nearby uncut patch. The shorter grass of the mown paths is attractive to butterflies, which benefit from varying grass lengths. Some birds, such as blackbirds and thrushes, also take advantage of the paths, which provide easier access when they forage for insects and worms at the edge of what must seem to them a 'forest' of impassable tall grass. The fourth advantage is to be able to set aside at least one area for late-flowering plants such as knapweed, betony and scabious. Not only are they a valuable, continuing source of nectar plants for bees and late butterflies, but they also provide a continuation of seeds for the birds, as well as some for me to harvest too. There is a slight contest as to who gets what they consider to be their fair share of the seed and the same minor conflict of interest occurs throughout the summer season as I hand-gather seed to add to my new meadow. Sorrel is so popular with the finches that I almost always miss my opportunity. But how consoling to know it is so much appreciated!

Seeds of local provenance

Saving local seed is vitally important. Environmentalists are urging us to help conserve what they term 'locally distinct character and diversity'. It is absolutely vital that seed is harvested from British stock but it is even better if the seed can be sourced and harvested from local meadows. There may be minute regional differences that may have great relevance; to a layman such as me this is mysteriously technical, but leaves me increasingly in awe of nature. I certainly welcome all the information available from conservation organizations such as 'Plantlife' and the

'Flora Locale' website (see page 157). I am willing to spend many happy hours harvesting seed and I am pleased to say the Davey Meadow has both received local seed and donated seed to foster the development of several small meadow projects in the Blackmore Vale, including contributing to my own newly created meadow.

Seed harvest

The first seeds to be harvested are those of the yellow rattle, which flowers in June and continues into July. The fat, rattling 'pods' are easy to gather, dry and empty so the large seed can, if necessary, be stored cleanly until required for sowing in autumn. Most other wildflower and grass seeds require slightly more attention to separate them from the seedheads and chaff (a wok is a useful piece of equipment when winnowing seeds). There are often multitudes of tiny insects that are inadvertently captured and need to be released. I store a proportion of the fully dried and cleaned seed in paper bags, sealed in airtight containers, in the fridge or at least in a cool, dry place, safe from mice and ants. Where possible though, I redistribute all the harvested seed directly into my 'foster-meadows' during the summer months; this is how it works in nature. Even though many seeds may remain dormant in the soil for months or even years, the germination rate of stored seed begins to drop off after eight to ten months. Sometimes the grass sward is too thick for the seed to easily find its way down through the mat of grass to reach the soil surface. With such conditions it may be sensible to delay sowing until the grass has had its final cut or has been grazed in autumn or even the following spring.

Sowing into turf

Seed sowing is a game of chance when you are trying to add to or increase flowering species in established turf. Only a small percentage ends up where it has an opportunity to germinate and successfully compete with the closely neighbouring plants. There will also be a huge seed-bank of grasses and wildflowers from the existing meadow and some species may not be our first choice. Dragging a set of heavy harrows over the site will create some seeding opportunities but this may be a bit Draconian and, indeed, impractical to arrange in a small meadow. A little agitation with a wire rake can be efficacious and it is possible to be far more selective in targeting specific areas. Meadows vary so much in size and character (I nurture some delightful 'mini-meadows' which are only a few metres/yards square – see pages 128-31) that it is difficult to make sweeping statements and maybe there is a limit as to how much we could or should intervene. There are times, however, when there seems to be no option but to try.

Controlling and replacing unwanted species

Sometimes it is the smaller, less obvious plants that threaten to hamper the chances of increasing the diversity of wildflower species in the meadow. In the Davey meadow, creeping buttercup was our *bete noir* and white clover can also be equally, if not more, menacing. It is hard for a young seedling of another species to pitch camp among such insistent, carpeting weeds. There were some patches where almost all other species were excluded by creeping buttercups, which revel in fertile, damp soil. Meadow buttercups (*Ranunculus acris*) enjoy the same conditions but they are a far more acceptable plant community member, having an innocuous manner of growth without creeping, rooting stems. It was difficult to alter these creeping buttercup-friendly conditions without radical action that would shake the balance of the other plants in the non-infested areas. I tried to remove the problem by digging, but this just stimulated germination of the ready store of its seeds or injected new vigour into the few bits of plant we managed to miss.

Turf-cutter mini-scrapes

We had more success when we hired a motorized turf-cutting machine and removed tracts of buttercup-infested turf, along with a certain number of their seed bank and the very fertile uppermost layer of topsoil. The turf-cutter can be set to a depth of about 5cm (2in) in order to lift the plant and most of its mat of roots. The resulting bare patches varied in size but were usually less than 1m (3ft) square. We then attempted some reseeding, sowing desirable species into the resulting spaces. Some of these mini-scrapes were sited in places where the surface water readily drained away so we could sow the seed directly once we had just lightly scuffled up the soil surface. In other places, the turf-cutter's scrapes left a bit of a crater where rain-water gathered and was slow to drain away. We could either capitalize on the situation and sow seeds of plants such as ragged Robin, which would benefit from the damp micro-environment, or we could fill the depressions with sand and then sow other species into a nutrient-free medium which would be relatively free of weed seeds. We tried both methods with interesting, varied, but limited results. Some of the mini-scrapes were planted with home-grown plugs or bare-rooted plants, which usually established well. The worst problem was from the remaining creeping buttercups seizing their chance to re-invade from the edges. Perhaps I should have been bolder with the size of the remedial patches? But then I would have been getting closer to 'scraping' rather than 'restoring' and I wanted to resist too much interference.

FOOTNOTE: I have since tried this method where the grassland is dominated by a mixture of native grasses, rather than creeping weeds, and results have been far more encouraging. I constantly experiment to see what can be achieved but, at the same time, I now put more and more trust in the steadfast system of management. Within limits, what turns up is probably there for a reason and there is undoubtedly some creature in the food chain which will thrive and help to support another. And so on.

Grazing

For us, the big shake-up comes in autumn and winter when we try to get the meadow grazed. Cattle are said to be best for helping to achieve species diversity. Sheep are useful if there is a thatch of grass debris. Horses graze patchily. Goats are browsers and not efficient as a mowing machine. We have both horses and goats so we have to try to make the best of it! We allow the two horses to strip-graze for short spells. This encourages them to graze much more efficiently. We take care to remove at least some of the droppings to avoid excess added fertility but bits are left to provide organic material to feed the soil bacteria and fungi. We invite the goats in if we want the hedgerows trimmed back, including the new growth of brambles, as they quest for new territory. The horses favour the grass above the broad-leaved plants, though it fascinates me how they manage to include an apparently measured amount of the valuable herbage with each mouthful. As they cavort about, they churn up, or 'poach', the land, when it is wet. This poaching (as mentioned earlier) is one of the spin-offs that come with grazing. Bare patches are created – like mini-cultivations – where the existing wildflower seed has an opportunity to germinate and the seedlings can get established without immediate competition from their mature neighbours. Seeds that may have lain dormant for many years can become exposed to light and other conditions needed to trigger germination. In wet conditions, it is also easy to add wildflowers plants to these small 'craters'. I sometimes even swap small pieces of flower-rich turf from one meadow to another, but I always keep the turf true to the locality. During bouts of very wet winter weather we have had to intervene when 'poaching' has become more like 'ploughing'. A certain amount of turbulence is acceptable but the turf structure must not be undermined. Too much disturbance from hefty sets of hooves can be detrimental so, as with all aspects of meadow management, a balanced, middle-way must be sought. We found that a solution was to limit the stock to occasional grazing during spells of slightly less wet weather.

Horses are not the ideal grazing animal but, with carefully timed and organized strip-grazing, my horse, Clary, plays an efficient part in our meadow-management, provided we remove the excess droppings.

Borrowed or simulated stock

There have been other times when horse grazing could not be arranged and we have offered free grazing to a local sheep farmer who brings his own electric fencing to contain his stock. This is a useful arrangement for anyone with a small paddock that has potential for developing as a meadow. In odd years when the grazing did not happen, we had to simulate the grazing and poaching. We mowed the grass aftermath in October and charged about the meadow during the winter weather, stamping foot-holes in the mud. I noticed passers-by didn't turn a hair – they are used to our eccentricity. Our combined efforts helped but, with an acre of ground to cover, a rugby team would have been a better alternative! It is certainly much easier and more efficient to let the grazing stock do the job.

The rich rewards

The Davey meadow has been a wonderful learning ground. We came to Sticky Wicket with the benefit of a traditional farming background but, had I not been fortunate in gaining valuable knowledge from expert botanists and ecologists, our project would be the poorer. To think, I might never have truly valued the umbelliferous corky-fruited water dropwort for the tongue-twisting little local star that it is. Or I might have wrongly believed it to be toxic, like its relatives, and regarded it with animosity. (The closely related hemlock water dropwort is lethally poisonous.) I would certainly have passionately admired the beauty of my exquisite sorrel but perhaps I wouldn't have realized how crucial it is to the small copper butterfly. With some traces of prejudice lurking from my agricultural past, I may have been slow to appreciate how stunning is the tall, shimmering, meadow buttercup (even though I cannot learn to love her creeping sister). There have been endless joys and discoveries already, and still a wealth to come. I have toyed with different ideas and methods, and enjoyed observing the results of our gentle experiments. In this account, I have explored and recounted most of the details of the aspects of management that I hope may be helpful to anyone interested in conserving the flora and fauna of the small 'home-owner's meadow'.

The successful restoration of this mature meadow helped to give us the understanding and incentive to venture onwards and create a brand new one on another part of our land.

THE NEW HAY MEADOW
(a   n e w l y   ' c r e a t e d '   m e a d o w)

This half-acre meadow has been made from scratch since 1997. Three to four hundred tons of topsoil were moved to form the mount where our goats now benefit from an (upwardly) extended surface area of grazing. The land divides our garden from our smallholding and forms a gentle transition between the two. With the installation of temporary electric fencing, grazing can be arranged for short spells but this is explicitly more of a 'domestic meadow' than one that could be even loosely termed 'agricultural'. This project was very much conservation led, our key interest being divided equally between the preservation of both our local flora and its inter-related fauna. Nevertheless, the fact that the meadow would also enhance our land with a consummate beauty was never for one moment sidelined!

In 1986 we acquired our bungalow and almost four acres of rough pasture. The soil is, as I mentioned earlier, a fertile loam over heavy clay between which a thin layer of gravel is sandwiched. In 1996 I described the original grassland thus: 'Years ago our land had been common ground. There was no evidence pointing to agricultural use other than grazing or hay-making but the land had been mismanaged in years prior to our arrival. The (then three-acre) field had been seriously under grazed or cut, resulting in a tangled 'thatch' of accumulated grass debris, which held water like a sponge. I suspect this land may have been treated with chemicals which had further undermined the biodiversity and

The New Hay Meadow lies between the wilder fringes of the garden and our smallholding. The spoil from the scrape had been usefully recycled to create the nearby 'mount' – a feature for our goats to enjoy and a place from which we can admire the local landscape.

resulted in just a handful of the least desirable plant species remaining and hardly any notable visiting wildlife.'

Our limited efforts

We rescued the land from this immediate set of circumstances by abstaining from using fertilizers or herbicides but, because of the required year-round horse grazing, it was impracticable for us to put the land back into a proper hay-meadow regime to help reverse the damage. Anyway, little did I know, it would probably have taken 20 years or more to even begin to see a significant reduction in fertility. We did the best we could, but 'horsy-culture' (in a small space) seldom goes hand in hand with the remedial treatment of grassland. However, we explored the potential by concentrating our energies into a few trial patches to try to discover a more effective method of restoration.

The nine-year offensive

We laid a simple drainage system to relieve the problem of some of the surface water. Then we set to work to tackle the docks, thistles and nettles with the help of our three goats. They nibble the tops and so help to prevent any future seed formation and they will also eat most plants that are cut and left to dry. By combining goat browsing with cutting and digging, we took control of these particular weed species but unfortunately the opportunist creeping buttercup soon moved into the spaces, so we just exchanged one problem for another. Most years we took a hay crop off part of the site. Our one horse grazed the land, which was metred out in increasing zones as we moved the electric fence to widen her territory in winter, and I did my best to pick up the droppings regularly to avoid compounding the fertility problem. We sectioned off small areas and tried various methods of reseeding – with hopeless results. In desperation, we even sprayed one experimental plot with glyphosate, before reseeding. It serves us right for momentarily abandoning our organic principles because the results were consistently disappointing. Whether we sowed into lightly disturbed or dug ground, or sprayed turf, exactly the same grasses and weeds returned and, with seemingly renewed vigour, overpowered the germinating seedlings of the newly sown species. Naturally we had never applied any fertilizer ourselves, but it is likely the field had been treated in recent years and the effect of chemical fertilizers can endure for many years, affecting the composition of both the soil nutrients and the micro-organisms it supports. The combination of fertile soil, a copious weed seed-bank, inadequate drainage and past mismanagement nevertheless conspired to defeat us after nine years of effort.

The turning point

We saw no encouraging signs to persuade us to persevere with an attempted programme of restoration. The pasture was not good for grazing stock; it offered only limited wildlife value and it did nothing to enhance the landscape. If we were to succeed in making a species-rich meadow in our lifetime, we realized we needed to do something radical to make the conditions favourable for establishing wildflowers and a desirable mixture of native grasses. The odds were stacked against us, as things stood.

Sound advice and inspiration

We were very fortunate to meet local landowner and avid conservationist, Clive Farrell. We visited his 100-acre property and were bowled over by the phenomenal success and outstanding beauty of his extensive wildlife projects that focused on restoring and creating woodland, wetland and, particularly, grassland wildlife habitat, where the interests of butterflies are foremost. Following his example and his advice, we bit the bullet and in 1997 we carried out the topsoil scrape. (The methods have been described in the section on meadow creation on page 34). It is a bit of an enigma for a farmer or a gardener to be persuaded to regard much-valued topsoil as 'the enemy', even with all the evidence before him or her. I must stress here that a scrape should not be lightly undertaken. It causes a certain amount of ecological disruption and one has to be convinced that the newly created habitat will eventually be of far greater worth than the original. I am glad we had faith in Clive, put prejudice to one side, and had the courage to proceed, for we are seeing astonishingly positive results in a very short time and I feel entirely confident that the end has justified the means.

Special provenance

Not only did Clive give us all the encouragement we needed, he also provided us with the generous – in fact, priceless – gift of seed from his own meadows. This meant that the new Sticky Wicket meadow would be 'a daughter' to his very local meadow, rich in wildflowers and on soil that is almost exactly like our own. Indeed the story goes back further. Clive had originally secured seed from an ancient meadow in a nearby secret, hidden valley where 'time had stood still' for centuries. Fifteen years ago, he had been granted permission to harvest some of the precious hay to begin a nucleus of seed stock on his land. He was pleased to hand a second generation of seed to me, just as I am thrilled to be able to supply small amounts of my third generation of seeds to initiate other local projects. I had also saved seed from the Davey Meadow and from local wildflowers gathered from the few remaining pockets of what used to be our water meadows and common land. The resulting mixture that I applied contained a very high ratio of wildflowers to grasses.

The changing flowering pattern
'For whatsoever a man soweth, that shall he also reap'; true, up to a point, but wild-flowers will only grow if and when conditions are right for them. A shifting species pattern emerges as the young plants try to sort out their domain, organize

themselves into 'tribes' and battle for supremacy as they build their empires. In the first year we added a small proportion of cornfield annuals to our seed mix. We deliberately applied our combined meadow and cornfield mixture at a low seeding rate – barely a gram per square metre (⅓ oz per square yard) – to encourage the strong, healthy development of the perennial plants. The cornfield seedlings helped anchor the shifting, fine-clay soil particles, acted as a nurse crop to shelter out tiny perennial seedlings and, in the meantime, gave us a glamorous and colourful tapestry of native plants. Cornfield annuals can germinate only in places where there has been recent disturbance or cultivation of the soil. They originally became established when Stone Age man first ploughed the land for growing grain and they existed in cornfields until the chemical revolution rapidly wiped out all but the occasional, enduring poppies. The flowers of the cornfield cannot exist in grassland once it becomes permanent. The corn marigold, corn poppies, corncockles, cornflowers and corn camomile bow out very rapidly, even though some of the seed stock will remain locked up for years to come. With the exception of one or two corncockles, our colourful array predictably disappeared after the first year. It was 'thank you and farewell' as their transitory role ended. The grassland perennials started to flower in the second year and the infant meadow began to show some indication of how it would look when mature. However, we are still experiencing a juvenile period when some surprising 'boom or bust' events can occur. Ox-eye daisies are most often an early pioneer species and we certainly had our share of these pretty flowers, but not a disproportionate number. In newly sown meadows they can seem an irrepressible force but, in fact, such plants eventually diminish in volume and gradually equilibrium is reached as other species take their place. Many changes occur as the plant community shuffles and reshuffles during the formative years and there can be some astonishingly beautiful flowering events as the meadow 'metamorphoses'. In our New Hay Meadow, nectar-rich hawkweeds were also among our early settlers and, together with the daisies, they made a fine matrix of yellow and white which drew in all sorts of nectar-seeking insects.

Although our damp conditions favour the growth of ragged Robin, we were mystified by such an exuberant rush of pink in the third year. This plant is on the list of endangered species so we will be able to pass on seed and help bring it back from the brink.

Deliberate or chance seedling?

It is strange how plants apparently 'arrive from nowhere'. In year three, we had an unprecedented abundance of ragged Robin, which created a fabulous pink haze above the developing later-flowering plants, such as knapweed and betony. True enough, the winter had been abnormally wet, but I could not account for such a huge volume of this seed having found its way onto the scrape. I am pretty sure disproportionate amounts of it had not been included in Clive's original seed mix; it may have happened because the hitherto buried, dormant seed was brought to light as a result of the scrape. It certainly confined itself to very particular patches which, curiously, were not necessarily the wettest, as one might imagine. One thing I regret is not having left a section of the scrape unsown so that I could see exactly what germinated from the land's own seed-bank. It would have made a fascinating comparison, although it would have been difficult to draw conclusions as to what had been uncovered and what had recently 'arrived': travelling on the wind, carried by birds or distributed by other of nature's remarkable agents. Seeds of some of the more 'mobile' species may be blown in, airborne by virtue of their ingenious aeronautical designs. Birds spread undigested seed via their droppings and some seeds travel attached to the bodies of furry animals. Insects play their part: for instance, ants carry seeds from place to place and eat the waxy coat of cowslips, thereby encouraging germination. As I pick up such gems of information, I wonder just how many 'secrets of the earth' remain unaccountable mysteries.

Yellow rattle

There was no mystery about the appearance of yellow rattle. I had sown generous amounts of fresh seed saved from the Davey Meadow. What was indeed remarkable was that I reckon that almost every seed must have germinated and each year (so far) the numbers continue to multiply. As with many wildflowers, the seeds need a period of cold weather to break their dormancy. If conditions are not favourable for them to germinate, they will soon disappear from the grassland because the seed is only viable for one season and the plant is an annual. The first year, when the other plants were still tiny, the meadow looked, at first glance, like a field of cowslips. Although my seed mixture had contained only a very small proportion of grasses, I wanted to be sure they would be suppressed – and remain suppressed – for as long as possible. Had I been in a rush to 'green-up' the site, I could be accused of actually over-doing the rattle because it was to be three years before we saw any sign of a significant grass sward developing among a sea of rattle and young wildflowers. But I was in no hurry; meadow making is not for the impatient or over-anxious. I wanted to allow plenty of time for the wildflowers to get well ahead of the on-going contest that undoubtedly lay ahead and the rattle was doing a good job of digesting almost all the grasses.

Watch, wait, relax, enjoy and share

I was quite at ease with my lean-look, juvenile meadow and certainly not looking to force an early result. The combined effect of the small proportion of grass sown and the widespread rattle gave me a relaxed time, management-wise. Up to that point, I had just tidied some of the flower stalks after the seeds had been left to ripen and fall or were gathered up and redistributed across the site. Where once I would have carted away ten or more heavy bales of substandard hay, I had removed just ten fluffy barrowloads of material, which was barely the equivalent of one compressed hay bale. It was bad luck on our stock but great news for our wildflowers and wildlife. It was also good news for my neighbours. We saved some of the trimmings, where ripe seed-heads were intact, and wheeled barrowloads down the road to spread on the ground where two new projects were in hand. The 'hay' was scattered, then left to dry and for the seed to be shed, before the debris was raked off. The consequence, hopefully, is that another generation of Dorset wildflowers will now happily proliferate there.

Local variations

In those early days, it was fascinating to watch an illuminating map of the land unfolding before us. The way the plants grew indicated the local variations in soil fertility and where the land lay especially wet or was stony and drier. The species varied from place to place, some growing in zones, interlocking one sort with another, with others weaving though all parts of the field and unifying the pattern. In the first year the greatest proportion of cornfield annuals, joined by red clover, grew lustily in a diagonal band that dissected the meadow. We think that evidence of an ancient hedge line had been revealed and that those particular plants were suited to that extra level of natural fertility that must have been locked up for years. We had never previously noticed any 'green anomaly' in the old pasture. This event reminded us to draw up an accurate plan and install the metre-/yard-square record grids so that we could monitor the present and future developments. I also keep regular photographic records.

Glory days

In the third year, the sensational flowering event drew garden visitors from the delights of the wildlife garden to our newly opened meadow. They would sit for a while on the rustic seat at the entrance and gaze across the idyllic scene before following the winding paths to the mown circle, where they would study the information board and often gather in enthusiastic discussion with other visitors. Captivated by the combined

Our garden visitors are captivated by the old-world charm of the meadow. Many question the disappearance of our flower-rich meadows and feel inspired to go forth and make their own.

charm of the flowers and the butterflies, the buzz of bees and the sounds of the grasshoppers, people were entranced by the experience. Some ladies were tearfully emotional: 'I haven't seen anything like this since I was a child!' was a frequent comment – from those of an age to remember. And, 'Whatever happened to our wildflower meadows?' was the next response. 'Yes, what indeed! We have been robbed', I would reply. It was most encouraging to see how many people discussed their attempts or intentions to try meadow gardening and then asked for advice. As it is too big a subject to compress into a short discussion on an open day at Sticky Wicket – and be at all helpful – I thought I would prepare a useful four-to-six page leaflet. It grew!

Media response
Our flamboyant meadow also attracted the attention of my friend, garden photographer Andrew Lawson, with the result that the meadow was featured in

books and magazines, and a fabulous photograph held a proud place in the Millennium issue of the National Garden Scheme yellow book. The meadow made its television debut, giving us a video archive. Records most certainly highlighted an encouraging and dramatic transformation from the gloomy days of Yorkshire fog and creeping buttercup! We may not see the likes of those early explosive events again but we should hope to see a steady settling down of an established plant community. It may eventually look more sober in comparison but, hopefully, it will become increasingly diverse and eventually the floral community will begin to stabilize. I hope it will always be conserved as a living example of the lost local flora and be a safe haven to at least some of the local and visiting fauna.

The legume effect

During the first year, grass vetchling, a vibrant grassland annual, was also very much in evidence in localized spots. As the name suggests, it looks like grass but has a curious, vivid pink pea-flower which, on close examination, tells you it is a legume. It is one of the few annual plants that can survive in meadows. However, in the second year, the vetchling was far less evident, although we noticed an increase in other legumes such as red clover, black medick and bird's-foot trefoil. This was good news for the bumblebees and the butterflies (respectively) but created a slight problem for us. After all the effort and expense of removing fertility, here were plants at work processing nitrates and feeding our soil via their root nodules. This was quite a serious spanner in the workings of my infant meadow. Even if we mowed the clover areas to prevent further spread by seed, the mowing would stimulate the vegetative growth of the plants. We can only hope that during the on-going plant community power struggle, the legumes' stronghold will be weakened or we can discover a way to subdue their exuberance if they become overbearing. The wood pigeons are showing an interest so perhaps they will be the controlling force. Clovers are said to favour soils that have a high level of phosphorus. Red clover sometimes gives up and dies out to some extent; more to be feared is white clover, which can be far more menacing and persistent. In spite of their disadvantages, the legumes are

Common bird's-foot trefoil, a legume, provides a constant supply of nectar during its long flowering period and is an essential food plant of the common blue butterfly.

all wonderful wildlife plants, provided they are the true wild species. I would happily 'accept our lot' and settle for a pink and yellow meadow if I could believe it would be a sustainable plant community that would not lead to skulduggery with opportunist, coarse, unwanted plants finding their way into the gradually enriched soil. We think grazing may control the legumes if the logistics of stock management can be arranged. At present, the scraped ground has not yet fully stabilized with a fibrous, established turf that is robust enough to withstand the excessive wear and tear of a boisterous young horse. I see a number of wood pigeons on the meadow so I hope, but cannot be sure, that they are eating the clover and doing both themselves and the meadow a good turn.

Dyer's greenweed

It was only in the third year that dyer's greenweed made its presence known. It was surprising that this leguminous plant eagerly took up residence in our wet ground.

There are mixed opinions about the preferred habitat of this shrubby plant but I am led to believe it favours chalk rather than wet clay. It is not a plant that is commonly found in hay meadows but it is no surprise how far and fast the seed spreads when I listen to the explosive sound of the popping seed pods. Under the traditional hay-meadow regime of a mature meadow, it would be cut during its flowering time (in July only) and its spread would be thereby seriously curtailed. It is a woody plant but nevertheless seems to cope with a harsh, annual cut, and regenerate with handsome, hale and hearty wands of fresh, bright green growth with vibrant, chrome-yellow pea-flowers. In 2002, my July diary entry read 'it seems as if, in the blink of an eyelid, my girly-pink, shimmering haze of pink ragged Robin has metamorphosed into a more laddish golden prairie!' Certainly, the sight was indeed spectacular but I did not want to be overpowered with the effect and I certainly wanted to avoid my other treasured plants being overpowered by a bully. When golden flowers turned to ominously plump black seed-heads, I set about cutting down most of the plants, either where more vigorous patches of meadow began to need mowing or individually where the plants stood head and shoulders above their companions. I think this was a wise move, bearing in mind the topsy-turvy way that new meadows develop when we create an inevitably unnatural, back-to-front order of 'evolution'. I have put myself in the challenging position of having to work out a certain amount for and on behalf of the plants I have taken into my care. What an awesome thought! Perhaps they would sort their lives perfectly well if I got on with mine and left them to it. Who knows?

An unfortunate mistake

There is one thing I did which I very much regret. There was one small corner of my meadow that had been sown with commercially available seed prior to the main operation. At the time, I was unaware of the tendency of some seed companies to include alien species in their mix of 'wild' flowers. Even if I had known this, I might not have registered the significant impact and disadvantages of growing non-native seed or wildflower species that have been hybridized to produce agricultural strains.

Dyer's greenweed, an uncommon, leguminous grassland plant, once harvested to produce yellow dye, has found exactly the conditions it needs to prosper in our young meadow.

I have only recently begun to learn the ecological implications. For example, the alterations to clover plants produced by hybridization meant that certain insects cannot access the nectar. Bumblebees are becoming serious victims of the loss of true wild red clover as a result of the inaccessibility of the nectar at the base of the lengthened flower corollas. Five species of these wonderful insects have been lost already and others are in serious decline. The alien agricultural clovers have hybridized with the true native species and overpowered their more delicate relatives by virtue of numbers and their oppressive growth. In my meadow I spotted some rather loutish red clover. There were also some obese looking trefoils, leggy medick and oversized ox-eye daisies that gave the game away. An unhealthy amount of Dutch (white) clover also appeared. My friends from Butterfly Conservation pointed out the truth about the agricultural and European invaders. Most of the seed companies are scrupulous in providing British native seed stock but one or two are not. I had previously attributed the variations to the patchy difference in soil fertility, but I was wrong. It is infuriating to be hoodwinked into believing you are creating a very special, ecologically valuable habitat only to discover it is 'sub-standard' or, in some cases, totally useless for the wildlife you struggle to conserve. I am horrified to think that hybridization might have occurred and contaminated my local stock. I will try to strim and remove the offenders to prevent further rape of the true meadow.

Other less welcome guests

As responsible landowners with livestock, living in a farming community, we need to be aware of any plants that are toxic. Death from poisoning is a real risk, especially with goats who like to 'test' plants to discover their potential. This 'eat-it-and-see-if-I-die' attitude is nerve-racking for the goatherds! There are at least two plants on our land that can cause major problems for livestock. Hemlock water dropwort usually lurks near the headland, where there is a nearby water-course. These plants are among the most spectacularly lethal of our British natives, so I make certain they are completely controlled where they can either be reached by stock or drop their heavy seed, which could be carried downstream in the water-course to neighbouring farmland. We also have occasional plants of ragwort that turn up in the grassland; it is also a nasty poison but animals generally avoid it when it is green. Sheep can and will eat it and survive – in the short-term. However, the accumulative toxic effect is irreversible. Other grazing animals much more rapidly sustain permanent liver damage and can die horribly. It is more poisonous (and palatable) when cut, dried and inadvertently incorporated into hay, hence the need for extreme care.

The ecological bonus to grazing

I wanted to try and make my meadow safe to graze, if only on rare occasions. The herb-rich grazing can be useful as a tonic to my stock and, in return for their treat, they supply a special ingredient that will help with the germination of additional plant species. The droppings have an eco-system of their own and are broken down by various invertebrates, bacteria and fungi that all play a part in the complex chain which forms the meadow community. For instance, certain soil fungi are necessary in order for some plants to germinate and these may be present only when the meadow has been grazed by livestock or perhaps where dung is spread. Of course too many droppings would be detrimental if they resulted in surplus fertility being supplied to the land, so I regulate the grazing times and remove some of the droppings if they seem excessive. I am prepared to put the extra effort into my meadow-making because there is both modern science and country legend to support these theories. The plant name 'cowslip' came from the word 'cowslop' because, years ago, someone noticed that the seeds germinated in cowpats. Now scientists can explain in some detail what our ancestors had rumbled but probably didn't think it necessary to agonize over as they sipped their cowslip wine!

Goats often prefer to browse the hedgerows rather than graze but they help out from time to time. A sprinkling of their droppings helps to feed the special soil organisms that are an essential part of the grassland.

Other meadow matters

It is sad to have to recount that it has been necessary firstly, to fight hard and, secondly, be defeated in our efforts to save two local meadows. In the one case, despite a local campaign and every attempt to explain the need to conserve, we were outnumbered and outmanoeuvred by those whose decision it was to destroy our small living relic of the history of our village. The only thing I could do was to save seed from the sites and rescue some of the plants before and during the 'landscape' operations. The two sites were quite different. The first was a small area of traditional hay meadow with a beautifully compatible, stable community of wildflowers including pignut, corky-fruited water dropwort, tormentil and sorrel. Wildlife abounded and one could enjoy the intimate delights from the close proximity of the footpath that dissected the triangular patch. It is now a dysfunctional football pitch. No wildflowers have survived; no wildlife wishes to visit; no sports are played on the soggy site. It is mown to within an inch of its life in the interest of what would appear to be 'tidiness'. I despair. It has been an unforgivable saga of events that has disclosed a lack of understanding of our natural heritage.

Full circle of orchids

The second local meadow area occurred in an unlikely way, really by default, and is more recent. This nearby field was stripped of its topsoil to provide for gardens surrounding newly built local houses. Inadvertently, a wonderful scrape was made and a most interesting flora began to evolve in the space of four years – living proof of the benefits of denutrification. Among the wildflowers, there gradually appeared a thriving colony of common spotted and marsh orchids.

Naturally, it was most distressing when many of these newly developing wildflowers came under threat. First of all, the new mains sewerage pipe work was put through the field, disrupting part of the original scrape. That was enough of a disaster but worse was to come when, two years later, work began to reinstate the field for grazing. 'Foreign' dock-infested topsoil was brought in and left in a pile ready to spread on most of what was left of the original scrape, which, meanwhile, had been developing into a botanically and ecologically very interesting site. Fortunately, one local woman, Felicity (Fizz) Lewis (no relation) had watched with interest the way the wildflowers were developing. She had also watched the pipe-laying works, and now saw the waiting pile of topsoil, at which point she invited me to give an opinion and become involved. We were given permission by the owner to rescue the orchids, some sedges, patches of bugle and ladies' smock. We carefully lifted the orchids with as much soil as possible, hoping to keep their essential associated soil fungi intact. Some plants where rehomed in Fizz's nearby wildlife garden, some were brought to Sticky Wicket and others were transported to some of my other nearby projects. We must have managed this relocation successfully because the orchids are now very happily established. In our new meadow, they are rapidly colonizing in our clay subsoil, which is akin to the conditions from which they were delivered. There was excellent news to follow; Fizz was later able to purchase the land with the chequered career. She is a very keen conservationist and knowledgeable meadow-maker so the future now looks bright for another precious two acres of wildflower and wildlife habitat. Some of the orchids can soon return home! In fact, seeds from my new meadow have already been transferred to Fizz's meadow from my last year's late-summer cut and there will be plenty more to follow from the Davey Meadow, and the New Hay Meadow. I like a story with a happy ending, though it rarely works out so well for meadows, and sadly there was no last-minute repeal for the other local victim.

Other additions

Apart from rescue cases I did not put any plants into the main part of the meadow until I could see what had emerged from the seed. In year three, I saw that betony, sneezewort, sawwort, fleabane and devil's-bit scabious were absent, although present in Clive's 'mother meadow,' so he invited me to harvest seed and to remove a few plants of those species. These have now been added and are beginning to supply a luscious amount of nectar to attract even more butterflies. While the sward is still thin and there are a few vacant spaces, the best opportunities exist to help additional species to take their place. At the same time, there is a small amount of unwanted Yorkshire fog seeding in from my meadow margins. I always execute the dual task of removing some of this, and any other unwanted species, replacing them with the desired species in one operation. It saves bending and digging twice! Sometimes I dig out the rejects and sprinkle a tiny pinch of seeds in the gaps. I did this, for example, with seeds of pepper saxifrage that I had gathered from one of my nearby 'foster meadows'. I believe it likes to take its time to germinate, so trying to grow it in pots is not an option for a disorganized nursery-person such as me. Autumn is the best time for sowing wildflower seed but in spring it is easier to see 'what is what', so I cover my options and save a little seed to use in March and April.

Bulbs

Traditional hay meadows would have been unlikely to have had bulbs planted in them, although a few may have strayed in from the field margins or nearby woodland. I have not yet included any in the scraped area but I have some bulbs in the adjoining Garden Meadow. I may well be tempted to plant some fritillaries at a later stage but at present I don't want to do anything that may restrict my options to cut or graze at any time when I see the need to do so. Grass management clearly must take precedence.

Grasses and their butterflies

Most of the general-purpose seed mixes contain common bent, various fescues and crested dog's-tail, with others added if the mixture is for specific soil types. If you buy seeds individually, or add extra ones, you have an opportunity to control the proportion and varieties of grasses sown. For instance, crested dog's-tail is a particularly attractive, fine grass which is perfect in a wildflower commune. It has immaculate flowerheads that remind me of neatly braided hair. Sweet vernal is the slender grass that gives hay its sweet, evocative scent and, being early flowering and short growing, it is perfect for even the smallest garden meadow. I constantly harvest and spread it from one meadow to another. Certain grasses, rough meadow grass (the name is a misnomer – it is, in fact, very delicate looking) and some fescues and bents, for example, are especially favoured by butterflies, including the gatekeeper, marbled white, small heath, and the meadow browns. In fact, several native grasses host the caterpillars of some of our most treasured butterflies. I have tended to vilify coarse grasses because they can be counterproductive to the establishment of wildflowers. In a young meadow, or in one which is receiving remedial care, they can be far too aggressive. Even so, the fact that the small skipper, wall and speckled wood butterflies lay their eggs in mature plants means that I allow my heart to rule my head and sometimes fail to control Yorkshire fog at the very time when I could, at least, prevent seed from setting. One year I had a wonderful colony of skippers so

The brilliant male common blue butterfly is basking on medick, one of the favourite food plants of both adult and caterpillar. With these needs satisfied, we hope to have a resident colony of blues.

the pest grass was vindicated. The next year, ironically, I had too much Yorkshire fog and very few skippers. I am trying to persuade it to confine itself to the field margins along with the tough, tussocky cocksfoot. Cocksfoot is one of the grasses which support certain skippers and ringlets, so I enjoy it for this reason as well as reflecting on the attractiveness of its flowers, held in dense clusters on long, naked, spreading branches. The whole flowerhead is reputed to look like a cock's foot but it puts me in mind of a stylized, miniature oak tree.

The meadow flowers

Six years into the project, there are about 40 species of wildflowers in the New Hay Meadow and its field margin (not including the shrubby hedgerow plants). We are still a long way off the 100 or more in Clive's 'mother meadow', but we are heading in the right direction. I am certainly not seeking a 'botanical collection' for numbers' sake, but rather for the wildlife that may depend on the floral richness of the grassland habitat. Although I continue to add new species, there will undoubtedly be seeds that will spring up from the original sowing or even from the soil seed-bank.

Wildlife-attracting yellow plants

There are several other yellow plants adding to the golden glow of the dyer's greenweed I have already mentioned. Bird's-foot trefoil grows in profusion and is an excellent butterfly plant, especially for the common blue which both feeds and breeds on it. I find it confusing to remember the identification of certain hawkbits, hawkbeards and hawkweeds; I just know they are marvellous nectar plants and I am often too dazzled by the flowers and their insects to check their credentials as carefully as I might. I do know cat's-ear has proved to be one of the easiest to establish and one of the most impressive-looking. I watched, among other insects,

clouded yellow butterflies feasting on these plants last year. Yellow on yellow – sensational! I haven't yet spoken up for dandelions because gardeners seem to hate or, at least, fear them but I can easily forgive their naughty ways. In a meadow, 'weeds' become redefined as 'wildflowers' and, as a nectar plant, dandelions are one of the very best. They provide for the early nectar-seeking insects, especially bees, which, in turn, pollinate our garden plants and food crops as well as our wild-flowers. (Who would not want to encourage them?) Towards the close of the flowering calendar, another yellow member of the daisy family, fleabane, is there to provide sustenance. The flowers are much favoured by the small copper butterflies (which will have laid their eggs, hopefully, on the earlier flowering sorrel leaves). Before I leave the subject of yellow, I must mention plantains. One spring morning I glanced across the meadow and did a classic double take: it appeared as if the whole half-acre was filled with a haze of yellow orchids! I was, of course, deceived – fooled by the vision of copious amounts of pale, powdery, yellow pollen on the black heads of the ribwort plantain. The vision of this quite common – and not very well-loved plant – appeared to me every bit as radiantly beautiful as that of any much revered rarity. I welcome both ribwort, hoary plantain (another beauty) and greater plantain for the seeds they provide for the birds. This is what meadow-making, indeed wildlife gardening, is all about – caring and sharing. Peter and I try to care for our wildlife and, my goodness, how we share the pleasure of watching them thrive.

The violet spectrum

It is noticeable how many insects are attracted to garden plants in the colour range that spans lavender, mauve, violet and purple, and merges into magenta. In principle, knapweed is a pretty enough plant to grace the border and I include it with the nectar-rich buddleias, verbenas, asters, monardas and phloxes in the violet zone of my Round (nectar) Garden. But in my organically enriched garden soil, knapweed tends to makes a somewhat gross mound of foliage at the expense of some of the later flowering stems. In the New Hay Meadow, by contrast, the foliage is minimal

Devil's-bit scabious is a 'crowd-pleaser' for wildlife and humans alike. It is an excellent insect nectar plant and makes an admirable contribution to the glamour of the late summer meadow.

and the plant is very floriferous for many weeks. Local strains vary remarkably, both in appearance and time of flowering. By collecting seed from different places, I have ensured a stock of plants to flower in succession over several months. Knapweed is much visited by a very wide range of nectar-seeking insects and then holds a nutritious store of quite large seeds for the birds. Brightly coloured burnet moths breed on the stems as well as feeding on the nectar. I am beginning to think that, in a limited space, a 'knapweed meadow' would be the most simple to achieve and a fabulous gift to wildlife. The slightly bluer devil's-bit scabious is another wonderful wildlife plant that also flowers late in the summer season. This beautiful plant, with its pincushion flowers, is very much at home in the garden and flowers generously, even in fertile conditions. When we say 'wildflowers need infertile soil', what we really mean is: in meadows, wildflowers need infertile conditions in order to hold their own space in competition with the grasses. I lift, divide and distribute the

scabious plants to my meadows and try to beat the finches in the race to procure a share of the seed. Tiny scabious plants will successfully compete with their rivals in the open sward of the New Hay Meadow, whereas, in the Davey Meadow, a good-sized planting of them is needed if they are to survive the competition. In the mature turf, existing grasses and plants will be likely to assert their senior position over a newcomer, so in this case 'size does matter'. This year I am concentrating on increasing my stocks of betony and sawwort. Betony is a wildflower that looks as beautiful in the garden borders as it does in the meadow (or vice versa, depending how you regard the two situations). Sawwort looks like a miniature knapweed and

The nectar from the wildflowers in our meadows is foraged by many insects, including bees; honey is one of the valuable by-products of a well-managed flower meadow, and a local beekeeper attends the hives in our meadow.

is one of the later flowers of the hay meadow. It also helps boost the food supply for September butterflies and the host of other insects on the wing at that time of year.

Hives and honey bees

The Sticky Wicket honey bees are fortunate to be able to fly between the garden flowers and those in the meadow, so there is a wide range of plants from which they can gather pollen and nectar. I have no bee-keeping skills myself, but a local bee-keeper attends his hives on our land. This is an excellent arrangement which benefits both men and bees. Honey bees are responsible for the pollination of 84 per cent of our crops, so it is a fantastic bonus to be able to protect them on land that has a great diversity of suitable plants, is free of chemicals and has a reasonable chance of being GM-free, at least at present. The hives are kept where they benefit from the shelter of the hedge, but not too close to the places where we regularly walk or sit.

Mown spaces for access

Naturally, we wanted to be able to walk among our splendid plants and closely observe and enjoy both the flowers and visiting wildlife. We needed to have maximum access with minimum disturbance to plants and wildlife. Winding paths look irresistibly inviting and define the places where we access the various parts of the meadow. They also help to discourage random trampling by garden visitors who are understandably keen to discover and enjoy the flora and fauna for themselves. We accentuate the curving nature of the path design to maximize the areas reached but, at the same time, minimizing the numbers of flowers sacrificed. The paths do no harm to the wildflowers – indeed rather the reverse – and the mown parts allow opportunities for certain plants to colonize more easily than they can in long grass. Some, such as the versatile selfheal, can flower at a height of 2.5cm (1in) or rise to 30cm (12in) or so. Happily for the bees and butterflies, this makes it a good survivor.

Shifting path positions and stopping places

We vary some of the path positions slightly each year. This rotation helps different plants first to get established and later have their chance to flower. (Remember the lesson from the fox track, mentioned on page 54?) In the Davey Meadow, where the sward is mostly very dense, I described how we mow 60-90cm- (2-3ft-)wide paths

Meadow brown butterflies are among 23 species of insect that visit the humble ox-eye daisy. This plant is one of the early pioneering species prevalent in young meadows.

with a ride-on mower. In the fine sward of the New Hay Meadow, just the narrowest of paths are mapped out with a strimmer. This way they look far more naturalistic, as if created by the wanderings of 'wild creatures'. To some extent this is the case, even though I count myself and my dogs among them! I keep a one-way system for visitors to avoid the need for passing places, but, since it would be frustrating for people not to be able to pause and sometimes gather together among the flowers to observe and discuss the wildlife, I mow a circular space for such events. This is about 4m (13ft) in diameter and defined with logs. Sometime we picnic in our 'magic circle' but most often I just lie there, peacefully, and gaze and listen in wonder and admiration. I believe circles can have a strange effect. For me this space has somehow become 'hallowed'.

Mowing with butterflies in mind

The mown paths and other spaces are also very advantageous for the resident and visiting wildlife that greatly benefit from the variety of levels in the grassy habitat. There are certain butterflies which particularly rely on the grasses and on the nectar-laden flowers because they need the varying grass heights to be able to perch, shelter, feed and breed. I always feel guilty when I pass through the meadow and cause an 'uprising,' as dozens of meadow browns are disturbed from their activities. On warm days they will be feasting and courting but on dull days, and in the evenings, they roost among the vegetation. Then their presence only becomes evident if I inadvertently cause disruption. Orange tips, ringlets, common blues, small coppers, small skippers and clouded yellows have also regularly visited the New Hay Meadow. Hopefully many of these will have bred in our grassy oasis. Gatekeepers, holly blues, large whites, small whites, green-veined whites, brimstones, small tortoiseshells, speckled woods, peacocks, red admirals, painted ladies and commas flutter across the meadow, occasionally pausing to forage for nectar, but are more inclined to favour the hedgerows and the tussocky field-margin habitat. Almost all the butterflies I have mentioned will also visit our garden and some of them particularly favour the garden plants as a nectar source. This can distract one from the fact that, almost without exception, they all need native plants on which to lay their eggs. The caterpillars need very specific food plants and garden plants are rarely a substitute. Certain white butterflies and cabbages are an exception. Unfortunate for vegetable gardeners, but awfully good luck for the whites!

From meadow to garden

The New Hay Meadow is integral with my 'wilderness' White Garden, with its small Garden Meadow. Most of the butterflies I have mentioned appreciate the dual benefit of our garden that is filled with as many nectar plants as an insect could hope to find in insect paradise. I freely admit my garden now takes second place to my meadows but I never lose sight of the fact that it has been very purposefully designed and created to attract and support wildlife. Buddleias, ice plants (more specifically *Sedum spectabile*), eupatoriums and *Verbena bonariensis* are butterfly favourites in our garden, but they also love phloxes, plants in the scabious family and many of the herbs. They like the nectar plants to be in full sun but with the benefit of some shelter, so I have had to juggle with all these specifications and dynamics, both in the design and layout of the garden and with the way the old hedgerows are managed and the new hedges, copses and scrub have been introduced – all very thought-provoking!

Hedgerows

Our eastern boundary hedge is ancient and comprised of an impressively great diversity of native plants. Management-wise, we are partly at the mercy of our neighbours, as it belongs to their land. Fortune has been kind to our hedge in recent years for it has been allowed to grow quite tall while retaining a good thick base. It is robust enough to withstand the great wands of brambles and the thrusting hedgerow plants that make it so appealing to wildlife, and it is a special haunt of gatekeeper butterflies and of rabbits. The latter are a mixed blessing. Although unwelcome in the garden, the rabbits can do comparatively little harm in the meadow and, in fact, contribute to the way the flora evolves. I do wish, though, that they would desist from grazing the flowerheads of my ladies' smock and depriving the orange-tip butterflies of their favourite plant.

English oaks

There are five magnificent English oaks on our property and I decided there was space for a few more. One of these has been planted on the edge of the meadow against the hedge. It grew from an acorn (progeny of one of 'the five'), but originally positioned itself in a most inconvenient place in the garden. Now, hopefully, we have secured the long-term future of that genetic stock and we trust it will one day support at least some – if not all – of almost 300 species of wildlife that depend on oaks. I will have to bear in mind, but forgive, the downside to oaks close to pasture: the green acorns are toxic to stock, if they choose to eat them. I may seem a little paranoid about poisonous plants, because animals generally avoid them, but you never can trust a goat to conform to the norm. As with all stock, the selective process works only if there are enough options and provided boredom (or bloody-mindedness) is not a feature of daily life. Again, mobile electric fencing can resolve the short-term problems of separating stock from no-go areas.

Floriferous field margin

On the few occasions when this meadow has been grazed, I have separated the stock from the field margins. This resolves any problems with toxic hedgerow plants and leaves an undamaged reserve for plants and wildlife. Primroses and violets grow on the banks and are good for butterflies. It is remarkable how certain plants favour a bank or ditch. On land such as ours, which often lies wet, extra opportunities are created for an increased range of wildflowers to colonize where the terrain and soil conditions vary. For instance, square-stemmed St John's-wort and lesser spearwort like our clay-lined ditches and, being quite small plants, gain advantage in having space to grow in hostile, clay conditions that most other plants shun. Garlic mustard, on the other hand, is more of a hedgerow plant and one on which the orange-tip butterfly depends. I have encouraged it and added home-grown plants to increase its territory and make up for the grazed-out ladies' smock. We have willow-herbs and red and white campions, which are good for moths whose caterpillars feed on the leaves or seeds, respectively. Cow parsley needs no encouragement. Beautiful as it is, there is a super-abundance of this very successful plant, which is threatening to exclude other plants from our hedgerows. However, it is here to stay and benefits a range of insects with an early supply of nectar. In my small and vital space, I feel inclined to cut it down after flowering to prevent more seedlings. There are several valuable bee plants I want to protect and encourage; plants such as red and white dead-nettle and hedge woundwort, which help make up for the nationwide shortage of bumblebee fodder. Although musk mallow can grow in open grassland, I find that, like the campions, it much prefers life on the field-edge. Vetches also do best where they can scramble among the woody plants that creep in from the hedge. In winter, I cut back some of the growth of brambles and suckering shrubs to keep a satisfactory balance between scrub and grass. The stretch of hedgerow is only 15m (17yd), so it is quite feasible to do the work by hand and I can therefore be much more selective than would be possible if we were to have the hedge cut mechanically.

Buckthorn for brimstone butterflies

On the western side of the meadow, a new boundary was needed to divide the meadow from my vegetable garden and nursery area. It is only a small space, just 35m (37yds) in length, but I particularly wanted to grow buckthorn for the brimstone butterfly. It is said to fly widely in search of its specific larval food plants, buckthorn and alder buckthorn. Nothing else will apparently suffice. True enough, I have often spotted brimstones tearing through the garden as if on a mission and I would like to slow them down and invite them to stay, but I have a problem: purging buckthorn (*Rhamnus cathartica*) grows best on dry chalk soils and alder buckthorn (*Frangula alnus*) likes peaty, acid soils. Mine is neutral and wet. Perhaps I should have tried both, but I plumped for the former of the two, which, I believe, is unfortunately the more poisonous. The plants are slowly getting established but need mulching with fabric to save them from competition from the more vigorous grass of my unscraped field margin. At the time of planting, in my desire to help the butterfly, I failed to grasp the potentially poisonous effect on livestock, so my security has to be extra tight with field gates and fencing. I just hope the beautiful brimstones will appreciate my efforts.

More meadow wildlife

Butterflies are the 'class A celebrities' of the wildlife garden and meadows but there are hundreds of other creatures to consider and make welcome. There are numerous species of grassland-dependent moths, often unseen because only a very small proportion, such as the forester moth and the five- and six-spot burnets, are day-flying. Seed-feeding birds also enhance our landscape, especially the enchanting and immaculate goldfinches, in their colourful haute couture. Yellow-hammers usually wait for their share of the bounty in winter. Bumblebees, honey bees, hoverflies and other buzzing insects provide the nostalgic summer sound effects, as does the ticking of grasshoppers – now fast becoming rare. These are the creatures we see and/or hear most conspicuously but there are literally thousands of tiny creatures that inhabit

grassland (provided it is chemical-free). Overall, we have seen foxes, badgers, rabbits, field mice, shrews, voles, slow-worms, frogs, toads, newts, bats, beetles, moths and spiders, and there are also millions of minute, often unseen creatures that are a vital part of the eco-system. Many of them live at or below soil level while some, such as spiders, are shy, discreet and hard to spot. Indeed, I am told that the health of our individual garden micro-environment can be judged by the size of the population of spiders. This is encouraging news, for, on dewy mornings, the early sunlight reveals a

Habitat boosters, such as this carefully constructed log heap, are a great help in providing extra homes for the many and varied creatures which love to live in, or close to, grassland.

light 'duvet' of cobwebs extending right across the meadow and garden. I often wonder how butterflies manage to successfully cohabit with such a daunting population of predators, but hopefully, there will be sufficient for all-comers.

Slippery customers

Frogs and newts breed in our garden pond but find their way into the cool, grassy sward, especially near the field margin where the growth is more vigorous. I get very nervous at strimming time and work slowly, cautiously and methodically. I have rarely seen slow-worms but this is not surprising. It is not in their nature to be conspicuous but I have discovered them in our compost heap so I feel sure they must also enjoy our field edges where there are specially constructed features in which to hide. Slow-worms eat slugs and snails (very useful!), and worms, so food is plentiful for them. The remarkable way this mass of wildlife has gravitated to the meadow goes to show how desperate is the need for sensitively managed, chemical-free grassland habitat.

A fantastic result

The result of this particular meadow project is quite overwhelmingly encouraging! Our half-acre of 'worst scenario' grassland has turned into a wildflower-rich paradise for wildlife and for human spectators. In spring we see a spectacular pink haze of ragged Robin and there follows a sequence of flowers that continues to dazzle us and draw in the mass of beneficial creatures that are such an asset to an organically managed garden. Even in autumn, a few flowers bravely continue to flower until the first rimy frosts arrive and silver-edge the remaining winter seedheads. I continue to introduce additional plant species to help conserve the local flora but most of the original plants proliferate with no help from me. Orchids are popping up all over the field, indicating they are satisfied with the soil eco-system, now recovering from the disruption of the scrape. With the tremendous head-start that the flowers have over the grasses, I am very optimistic about the future of our meadow and look forward to watching it continue to flourish and mature.

Our healthy, ever-increasing population of common spotted orchids is a good indication that our land is in good heart and there is a promising way ahead for a diversity of wildflowers to form a thriving plant community.

THE GARDEN MEADOW

The site

There is an L-shaped, 60 x 6m (66 x 6½yd), grassy fringe of land that defines – or rather 'feathers the edge' of – my garden. This small strip of garden meadow is part of my outer 'white wilderness' garden, which is the last of four garden areas, each with a different focus of wildlife interest and contrasting planting style. The White Garden is particularly rich in fruits and berries, with grassy tussocks and shrubby thickets for wildlife habitat. I have used ornamental and native grasses as an integral part of the planting. My plan was to design and plant my garden to make it appear to melt imperceptibly into its surrounding agricultural landscape and the Garden Meadow helps to smooth the transition between this garden and my more recently created New Hay Meadow beyond.

The vision

I had a romantic image in my mind when I first began to make the White Garden. I dreamed of including a small meadow where the wildflowers would be mixed with selected garden plants and bulbs, imitating a medieval flowery mead. The paintings and tapestries depicting flowery meads were rather stylized images of richly flower-spangled turf and there must have been a large degree of artist's licence involved in the portrayal. I realized this, of course, but remained starry-eyed as I visualized my interpretation, which would contain predominantly white flowers. I planned to grow a matrix of native plants and grasses into which I would gradually naturalize some of the white-flowered garden plants and bulbs that I considered would look appropriate, beautiful and, at the same time, would be of benefit to wildlife.

The reality

The vision has more or less become a reality and I think it is, unquestionably, my favourite way of growing garden plants. But my dream was not realized without blood, sweat and tears and an on-going challenge to suppress the vigorous growth of the competitive grasses, which tended to overpower the broad-leaved plants. My experiences with this strip of grass turned out to be highly relevant to the way we approached and managed what was to be the later project on the site of the New Hay Meadow just beyond. I tried every trick in the book (if only one had been written) when I began the project about 10 years ago. I faced the worst scenario for meadow-making because this strip of grass was on very fertile loam where Yorkshire fog and creeping buttercup held dominion over all other plant species with the exception of a few docks, thistles and nettles. My ambition was to turn it into a wildflower meadow of the sort that so many of us dream about – flowery, fluttery and romantic. Although I had spent half my life looking after grassland of every sort, I had never needed to force the wildflower issue in this new way that lay ahead. I was about to embark on a frustrating yet fascinating voyage of discovery.

The small Garden Meadow has a mixture of predominantly white wildflowers and naturalized garden plants, which, after much trial, error and hard graft, we have successfully persuaded to grow in rich, loamy, clay-based soil (the New Hay Meadow is in the distance).

First abortive efforts

At first I was misguided enough to think that I could get a successful result by digging up the unwanted weeds and resowing with an appropriate seed mix. I even thought I might succeed by just scattering this wildflower seed into the existing grass sward (provided I then managed the grass in the traditional hay-meadow way). I must point out that I had done the best I could to make conditions favourable for the seeds to germinate. Having dug out the docks, thistles and nettles, I cut the grass so short it was nearly scalped. Then I scarified the turf quite hard using a heavy rake and an old potato ridger to disturb the surface. In principle, it is a method that is sometimes recommended and, had the soil been less fertile, it might well have worked. It did not! The grass grew back with a vengeance and soon overpowered the few struggling seedlings. Apart from the problem of over-fertile soil, the actual types of grass were complicating the issue. The species were too robust and the high content of Yorkshire fog made hostile conditions for seedlings trying to gain a foothold. I clearly needed a more open sward with shorter, finer-leaved grasses.

A second offensive

A more radical approach was necessary. I tried various ways of killing the turf so I could – as I thought – eliminate the problem grasses and buttercups. One way was to smother the grass and exclude all light. I tried covering some areas with black plastic and some with old carpet, which were left in place for a year. This certainly caused it some discomfort and at the end of a year it indeed had the appearance of dead turf so we were fooled into believing that just might be the end of the Yorkshire fog and creeping buttercup saga. Not a bit of it! The same plants bounced back with alacrity once the cover came off – the seed-bank took care of that. There were probably generations of dormant seeds waiting in reserve and light triggered their germination in a flash.

The wood-mulch theory

In some places I tried to prevent the resurgence of seedlings by covering the dead turf with a heavy mulch of wood-chips. This, in theory, would have an extra benefit of reducing the soil fertility as its nutrients would be used up in the process of their decomposition. I achieved a degree of success and the regrowth was effectively checked but I couldn't afford the materials for the whole area and, being 'a woman on a mission', I was anxious to progress with the planting rather than watch wood-chips decompose for a year or more! (It has been noticeable how well cowslips have colonized in the places where the densest layer of wood-chips was spread.)

The patchwork planting trick

I proceeded by fair means and foul until I had a 'brownfield site' in at least parts of my problem strip. Next I tried laying a ryegrass-free turf on top of the dead grass. This turf was composed of suitable fine grass species such as fescues. I now realize that turf may include modern grass hybrids which may have limited value to wildlife, but regrettably this did not occur to me at the time. However, this grassy covering helped to fool the underlying, dormant seeds for just long enough for me to establish some wildflowers using a combination of a patchwork of turf, plants and seed. I cut the turf into squares and triangles and laid it quite haphazardly with gaps varying between about 5-23cm(2-8in) apart. In the biggest gaps I placed wild-flower plants which I had grown in 5-10cm (2-4in) pots. In other places I planted small wildflower plugs. I then sprinkled wildflower seeds onto the remaining bare earth. I included yellow rattle to help suppress the grasses. Almost immediately there were encouraging signs and many of the wildflowers became established. I had been cautious in selecting seeds of species I knew to be robust enough to compete with the anticipated vigorous growth of the grasses.

The positive results

Every year we saw changes – for better or for worse. On the plus side, some wildflowers, such as knapweed and sorrel (two excellent butterfly plants), have proliferated most encouragingly. I tried to grow white knapweed from local seed, but each plant turned out to be mauve. Perhaps I was pushing things too far but I had hoped to harbour some unusual white forms of wildflower as a point of interest. A patch of white ragged Robin established well in one of the wood-chipped areas but gave up the ghost when I tried to shift some of them into the grassy ruck. Locally sourced white yarrow was easier to introduce and this is another good nectar plant and herb. Into the earthy gaps I sowed seed from the three umbellifers – corky-fruited water dropwort, wild carrot and pignut. At first, we had a spectacular two years when wild carrot was dominant. Unfortunately, this beautiful plant is one of the grassland 'pioneering species' which tend to diminish in numbers over the years. (The same is true of ox-eye daisies). The corky-fruited water dropwort was far better able to persist although I help it along by spreading extra seed after the final grass cut in October. The pignut spectacularly failed, but I have now arranged to take seed from the local cemetery, having persuaded our friendly grass-mowing contractors to allow a patch of it to flower. Once established, it is very inclined to grow in this area, if only allowed a chance. So, there was my existing and proposed matrix of predominantly white wildflowers!

The less positive results

The downside was the increasing dominance of certain grasses (including Yorkshire fog, which had crept back in despite our best efforts to restrain it with timely cutting). Creeping buttercups also began to forge their way back and the battle with these plants and the soil fertility is on-going. I regularly dig out some of the most brutish buttercups, and put my own fine grass and wildflower mix in their place. I also add some plants and these need to be well grown-on if they are to keep their place as a newcomer. Plugs are often recommended but I find they soon get swallowed up in the mass of grassy vegetation. I valiantly try to subdue the grass in various ways. Mowing it in June when it is at its most verdant is the best technique but, by doing this, the very wild-flowering event you seek has to be sacrificed in the short term, even though the perennial wildflowers themselves will suffer no ill effects. If I have a particular problem area, especially during a wet summer, I may have to make the sacrifice and carefully strim down the offending patch. It is obviously wise not to let it set seed.

Wildlife considerations

Mowing the grass early may, however, have adverse effects on some of the wildlife. For instance, some of the meadow butterflies will have laid their eggs on the grasses and these will be inadvertently cleared away when the grassy debris is picked up. It

If you peer into the grass sward, it is like a picture gallery of a million images. Even common plants such as buttercups show their splendour in the right setting. This meadow buttercup grows taller and with more elegance than its creeping relative.

is absolutely essential to remove the debris but best to leave it in place for two or three days for some of the insects to crawl into the underlying or nearby turf. Frogs and newts migrate from ponds to damp, dense, grassy habitats and are very vulnerable to the action of mowers or strimmers. Field mice and other creatures nest in long grass. There is a minefield of hazards that just go to prove how very much our wildlife values our grassy garden habitat.

Complications with bulbs

Mowing times can be further complicated if bulbs are involved. I planted snowdrops and wild narcissus about two years into the project but, with hindsight, I should have waited several years to be sure conditions were right and the lush grass-growth had fully abated. Were it not for the bulbs I would have the option to mow lightly once in spring (early April) to try and reduce the competition from grasses and help the flowers to compete with them. It has often been necessary to give the grass, where it grows with such virility on this unscraped edge, a spring cut. Dodging bulbs is tiresome and leaves the meadow looking as if the council mower-men have paid a visit! The narcissus bulb foliage tends to create a microclimate where the grasses are encouraged to grow tall in their shelter. Actually, I find the grasses are then quite easy to pull up if I can find a moment to tug at them. Of course, the grass growth also varies considerably according to weather conditions. I must say I have had moments when I have regretted my decision to plant bulbs as generously as I have.

Balancing decisions and methods

There are also the early-flowering wildflowers, such as ladies' smock and cowslips to consider. Only the most hard-hearted meadow-maker could mow those pretty heads off! It can be a tough call to make decisions about mowing. However, I try to find a middle way and employ (yet again) a 'patchwork' mowing system so that only a small proportion of the area is targeted at one time. Admittedly this disrupts the appearance a little, but by mowing winding paths, circles or other smooth shapes, I try to make my remedial work look as if it is part of the design. During the autumn, winter and early spring I regularly pull, dig or otherwise bully the grass and this helps considerably — especially if it is closely followed by the addition of alternative seed. Yorkshire fog, the worst offender, is an easy grass to identify, even in winter. Its soft, greyish foliage is distinctive. I make a point of digging out as many tufts of it as I can during the autumn. Again, I quickly sow any bare patches that occur with my harvested yellow rattle and 'quick-fix' corky-fruited water dropwort, which germinates very readily. Year by year I see encouraging progress as the ratio of flowers to grass alters favourably.

Rattle to the rescue

In this respect, my best friend and ally, yellow rattle, comes to the rescue. It has worked miraculously where I have been able to get it to germinate and survive in the first place. This manual thinning and harassment of the grass helps the seedlings to find a pitch. It can be tricky to persuade this pretty plant to stay 'on the case' and to ensure it keeps its place. I always harvest some of the seed to keep in reserve and add it to the areas most in need, and also scatter it generally, after the final cut in October. It germinates best from autumn sowing and loses its viability if stored for over a year. I avoid sowing it too close to the worst patches of creeping buttercup because by hampering the grasses, the buttercups then gain advantage and progress sideways unchallenged. The vagaries of rattle need to be understood, but it is well worth the investment of effort; gradually the grass growth is subdued and the wildflower magic can begin.

Garden plant introductions

By trial and error I discerned which wild plants would have the guts and tenacity to stand up to the native grasses. This information could then be translated when choosing some garden plants to naturalize among the natives, and led me to judge which would look glorious and fitting in their semi-wild status. In this respect the geranium family have excelled, especially forms of *Geranium pratense* which, of course, are designed for the job! The white forms of *Campanula lactiflora*, *Centaurea montana* 'Alba' and *Galega officinalis* 'Alba' have distinguished themselves by having the necessary competitive edge for surviving in a fertile grass sward. *Veronicastrum album* is the most recent introduction and seems to be coping well in a sea of late-summer grass. *Saponaria officinalis* 'Alba' takes a surprisingly long time to get established but endures well when it does and the same is true of *Valeriana officinalis*. There is no reticence on behalf of *Eupatorium cannabinum* (hemp agrimony). These three latter plants have distinctly pink overtones for placing in a purist's white garden but their virtues in feeding butterflies and moths encourage me to over-rule my artistic sensitivities. I could have put all these garden plants in right at the beginning but I wanted to set them into a matrix of wildflowers rather than allow them ascendancy in the formative years.

The learning game

The experiment goes on; I enjoy the work involved and find it a fascinating study-ground. My Garden Meadow certainly has its sensational moments as it continues to go through the long process of metamorphosis. As a wildlife gardener, I cannot really fail with this enterprise because, even if the grasses were eventually to dominate the flowering plants, I would still have a valuable strip of wildlife habitat where legions of grass-dependent insects as well as birds, field mice, shrews, voles, slow-worms, frogs and newts can shelter, breed and feed. Most importantly, I now understand the nature of my land and the challenge of trying to negotiate with it.

Our soil has an exceptional natural fertility which may well have been 'chemically enhanced' before we came here. Chemical fertilizers and herbicides upset the whole balance of the plants and the soil beneath them. Only in recent years have we begun to learn to what extent. If I had started with poorer soil and the wisdom of hindsight, this project would have been a lot less work. I have to conclude that I could have made less work for myself in the long run had I removed the original turf with the top few centimetres (inches) of topsoil. In the long run, it might also have been kinder to the wildlife I am struggling to conserve, too.

It has been a great challenge to achieve and sustain this beautifully blended tapestry of plants. With both plants and wildlife in mind, we needed to make very carefully balanced judgements, both while initially setting up the project, and then with the annual management procedures.

SMALL GRASSLAND PROJECTS

I N THIS CHAPTER I describe some of our small, garden-sized projects where wildflowers are grown in grass with varied plant and wildlife habitat in mind. For instance, I have used various materials to create drier and less fertile conditions than my own clay/loam soil. I take my lead from the varied local soil types and habitats that I closely watch as I regularly ride or walk the local bridleways and footpaths. I rely on the knowledge and instincts that come from continual observation and practical involvement, and I work on a tight budget and fairly limited space. None of my little plots is more than a few square metres (yards) and most projects could easily be squeezed to fit into all but the very smallest of gardens.

The Frog Garden Lawn

The original Frog Garden lawn was formed from the remaining space after the sinuous shapes of the borders and pond had been carved out, its turf ccomposed of the field grasses that existed before the house was built. The underlying soil lay extremely wet in winter because this lawn is on the lowest point of our land. The mixture of coarse and fine grasses and 'weeds' produced a patchy appearance but was not disruptive enough to disturb the overall effect I wanted to achieve. We had made no attempt to improve the lawn in the conventional gardening sense because at least it was consistently green for twelve months of the year and it suited our style of garden: I have never been interested in immaculate lawns. As long as these are green and luxuriously soft to walk on, the 'weeds' are welcome, although I prefer their flower colours not to be conspicuously at odds with those in the borders.

Lawn weeds
Creeping buttercup and white clover were the dominant lawn 'weeds' – as some

Even the tiniest meadows will attract and help support a wonderfully interesting and attractive range of beneficial wildlife. This burnet moth is feeding on a tufted vetch growing in a small patch of meadow just 3m(10ft) square and there are hundreds of other insects and mini-beasts in the plot.

might pronounce them to be — and both are notoriously difficult to eradicate. I was certainly not about to beat myself up by engaging in the sort of conflict required to produce a bowling green lawn! Dandelions appeared in places and I was quite at ease with their glowing presence. They are one of the very best nectar plants and I soon began to love my colour-enhancing yellow-spangled lawn which complemented the yellow-dominated colours of the Frog Garden. Even the creeping buttercup was acceptable in this situation. I had fought it hard and long in almost all other places but I knew when I was beaten; mown grass growing on naturally fertile and damp soil is buttercup paradise. It is best to give in gracefully, grit one's teeth and try to see its virtues: 'a bonny little plant which never lets you down and must surely give joy to certain insects'.

Changing the style and use

I was reasonably content with this open patch of mown grass for several years. This motley lawn was a good place for our three young dogs (and visiting children) to play but as they grew older they became quite happy tripping along the many mown paths which form the infrastructure of most of the other garden routes. I toyed with the idea of allowing the grass to grow longer and then close-mowing a pattern of paths to form shapes that complemented the design. This worked reasonably well but looked a little fussy until I simplified the design to dissect the lawn with a single curved path and to have similarly close-mown border edges. This effectively left me with two grass plots ripe for development!

New incentive

Recently I have devised a project to see if I could increase the biodiversity of my hitherto acceptable but rather bland, weedy lawn. I took my inspiration and lead from a local site. In fact, it could not be more local as only a broad span of native hedgerow divides my Frog Garden from this local graveyard. For 16 years I have noted the wildflowers in this extension to the old churchyard. I have seen — and sometimes suffered watching — the effects of the way it has been managed by various contractors who have blasted away with strimmers and mowers irrespective of any wildflower that may have raised its pretty head. Many wildflowers are wonderfully adaptable and can flower, between cuts, in grass growing at variable heights. Some, however, will give up the ghost while others will live on in a vegetative state without ever having a chance to flower and make seed. At last we have a father and son team of contractors who understand and respect the countryside, carry out an efficient job sympathetically and will mow round the flowering patches of plants such as primroses, speedwell, and bugle. They have kindly agreed to leave a few prime wildflower patches for other, taller-growing plants to show their splendour and allow me to collect seed so that I can perpetuate the local flora in my private 'plant reserves'. I hoped there would be some positive reaction from the locals when they saw the wonderful sequence of flowers that appeared like a Phoenix rising from the ashes but so far there seems to have been no response. How strange . . . the ethereal ring looked most beguiling.

'Horses for courses'

Anyway, from these spectacular flowery patches – the largest is only a 2m- (6ft-) diameter circle – I have saved seed of sorrel, quaking grass, pignut, lesser stitchwort, knapweed and devil's-bit scabious for my hay meadows, and prunella, medick, bird's-foot trefoil, cat's-ear and rough hawkbit, which are adaptable to varied habitats and management regimes. However, some plants flower best where the grass is shorter and the ground is better drained. Speedwell, for instance, particularly enjoys the conditions that have arisen as a result of chunks of clay being left mounded on top of some of the burial places after the excavations. I call them the 'spooky humps'; they are made all the more ghostly looking when covered with a blue haze in spring. Our caring contractors strim the uneven ground, diligently avoiding the speedwell and thus allowing them to have their moment of glory, which they share with the primroses.

Divide and conquer

I decided my two targeted Frog Garden patches would be made to differ. While I would allow the lower plot to remain unchanged and wet (though florally enhanced), on the slightly higher ground I would build my own version of the 'spooky hump'. I would then be able to grow low-growing wildflowers that favour the better-drained conditions and survive a part-time but regular mowing regime. By doing this, I would hopefully end up with both wet and dry versions of a flowering lawn.

Floral enhancement of the wet ground

I dealt with this original ground very simply by digging up some of the coarser tufts of grass and putting ajuga, selfheal, bird's-foot trefoil and silverweed in their place. They would join the few dandelions and celandines that were there and the whole jolly lot would have to battle it out with the creeping buttercup and clover. Ground ivy is less able to cope with a mowing regime but it survives well in the shadier area beneath a nearby tree, where the grass is thinner. I have also sown seed of the dandelion-like cat's-ear, which is beginning to compete with the others. So far, so good; a quietly colourful tapestry is beginning to complement my borders and is no problem to maintain. The most difficult part is deciding exactly when to mow because inevitably some flowers will have to be temporarily sacrificed for the survival of the whole community. It is the same old story; if the grass is allowed to grow too long or become exuberant, the poor wildflowers will retreat. I have to make a careful assessment and then take a firm decision.

Construction of our 'spooky hump'

Work began in autumn when it was dry enough for carting materials on to the site and just ahead of the wet and cold weather, which would benefit the project as winter progressed. The area is triangular in shape (so not so spooky after all!) and about 15 sq m (18 sq yd) in size. We needed to form a barrier between the underlying fertile soil and the infertile substrate we would use to form a smooth mound. We used a sheet of horticultural fabric although we could have used old carpet had there been any available. We were fortunate to acquire some rubble from the demolition of a local barn, which had been built using a combination of limestone, brick and flint. We spread the larger stones in the centre where the height was to be an optimum of no more than 60cm (2ft). Then we used the smaller ones round the edge of the triangle. The combined crushed mortar and a small amount of fairly lifeless-looking soil, which had sifted through to the bottom of the stored rubble heap, was used to cover the graded stones and help make a smooth top layer. To finish the job off to make it satisfactory for seed sowing and subsequent mowing, we topped the mound

The Frog Garden with flowering lawns. The contrastingly wet and dry conditions of each patch allow increased opportunities for planting a wider range of wildflowers than normal.

with a thin 'icing' of crushed limestone. (Sand, fine gravel or kibbled chalk would have done the job equally well; the point was to use a fairly fine substrate that was free-draining and free of nutrients.) We allowed a few days for settlement between the phases of the construction work. The next stage was to lay a patchwork of ryegrass-free turf. I could have just sown an appropriate grass seed mix along with my wild-flower seeds but I needed to give the mound some substance and stability to prevent erosion occurring during the winter months. We laid single strips of turf right round the edge of the triangle and then cut the remaining pieces of turf into rough and varying shapes and sizes, and laid them in a fairly random pattern in the remaining space within. Gaps of equal proportions were left between the bits of turf and this is where most of our precious plantlets and seed mixture were sown.

Saved seed and prepared plants
I began seed-saving the summer before the construction of the project and continued adding to this first sowing with freshly harvested seed in subsequent

years. Throughout June, July and August, I visited the churchyard every few days, in dry weather, to try and ensure the seed was harvested when fully ripe but before the birds robbed me of my share. I particularly wanted the yellows of the mini-dandelion-like lesser hawkbit, which is fairly low-growing, bird's-foot trefoil and medick, and the pretty blues of germander, slender speedwells and prunella, as well as daisies, which had never hitherto prospered in the original soggy ground. I tried to sow the seed immediately, following nature's timing of dispersal. However, if I needed to save an extra supply of seed I made sure it was quite dry before storing it in the fridge in a paper envelope. I sowed some of the seed in trays in order to have at least a few plants to kick-start the development of the flower-rich grass sward.

Plant and seed sowing

I filled a barrow with sand and added just a tiny amount of tired, recycled potting compost and some leaf mould. I used this to help bed in the young plants and give them a start in life. I set these infant plants in position, placing the smaller ones in the centre of the bare limestone-topped patches and the more robust plants near or directly into the turf. Finally, I stirred my seed into a bucket of the sand/soil mix, making sure it was evenly incorporated, and scattered three-quarters of it into the bare patches on top of the crushed limestone; the remainder I brushed into the turf. My part of the work was done for the year and it was for nature to do the rest. Rain and frost would further settle the ground and determine the fate of the seeds.

Management in the formative years

The mound needs to be regularly mown but allowing times when the low-growing wildflowers will bloom. We have to play it by ear, especially in the formative years when flowering may have to be partly sacrificed if the grass manages to grow too vigorously, despite the infertile conditions. In time, I think its vigour will become depleted on the starved ground and the wildflower threshold will increase, especially as I will continue to add the locally harvested seeds throughout the summer. I will also be planting some low-growing bulbs such as snowdrops and wild narcissus. The project is just one year old as I write and looks extremely promising. We cut it four times in its first season, with the mower set on its highest cut. The only problem we had was the need to carefully 'minesweep' the area for baby frogs, which were enjoying the new habitat as a perfect 'play school'! To have rashly mown without checking and lifting them to safety would have had unthinkable consequences. After all, it is their garden!

The Bird Garden Lawn

Our Bird Garden could boast having the smartest of our mown grass, albeit still part of the original field turf, comprising native grasses and a super-abundance of white clover. As my flower colours are predominantly pink, I might have achieved a sophisticated 'designer effect' were the clover pink! However, pink (or red) clover does not lend itself to survival in grass that is mown each week during the growing season. I can easily close my mind to aspiring to reach extraordinary aesthetic heights and happily settle for the fairly inconspicuous white flowers which the bees love as much as pink ones.

The green carpet
I have never had a problem with white clover in lawns. It is soft and springy to walk on, provides consistent evergreen foliage with small, neat, leaves and requires no fertilizer of any sort to keep it healthy. The nitrogen-fixing roots obligingly generate a natural source from the soil. The result is a perfectly self-sustaining, attractive, evergreen, hard-wearing, easily maintained and wildlife-friendly green carpet; what more could you want?

Getting the measure of clover
It is as well to be pragmatic and recognize the many qualities of the multi-talented white clover because it is one of the hardest wild plants with which to engage in contest. Sadly this can result in thousands of gallons of most unpleasant chemicals being repeatedly applied to some amenity grassland. It is as well we can so easily and rewardingly give it a home in our garden lawns, although it is not ideal in wildflower meadows where it can easily out-compete the other plants and over-enrich the soil.

'Weed' selection

The clover is reluctant to share its stronghold with other plants and as a lawn component this is a bonus because it tends to close all the spaces where broader-leaved wild plants might otherwise colonize. Among the soft pink and plum colours of the Bird Garden, the strong yellows that are so integral to the Frog Garden would clash most stridently. In this case, my much-loved wildflowers most unusually become 'offending weeds' and I dig up and compost the few dandelions that manage to stray in, along with the plantains. There are a few patches of creeping buttercup that I try to remove, and the clover seems to wait in readiness to move in when it recognizes its main competitor is disadvantaged.

Bird appeal

I am not sure exactly what it is about this roughly 126 sq m (150 sq yd) lawn which makes it so particularly perfect for birds – probably a combination of factors.

Obviously, because it is free of chemicals it supports huge numbers of invertebrates, but I wonder how much this is also to do with the dense covering of clover or the fact that the crescent of lawn is close to well-manured borders, which sometimes benefit from a little extra watering in very dry weather. If some of the water inadvertently spills on to the lawn, I make no apology when I see fine, speckled thrushes, blackbirds, robins, dunnocks and pied wagtails foraging for worms and insects in the soft, penetrable turf. Starlings ensure we never have a pest problem with leatherjackets in spite of the fact that our property is built on what used to be called 'Crane's Meadow'. Our few wood pigeons, which feed on the clover, seem to keep it 'pruned' in just the right proportions to help with the very minimal organic management. We never close-mow this lawn or any of our mown grass and even in times of drought they are always green and healthy.

Mole invasion

Even in a wildlife garden, moles manage to make themselves unpopular by undermining plants in the borders and making the lawn unsightly. My brother-in-law, a farmer, gardener and countryman like my husband, is skilled at fathoming out the moles' underground system and effectively setting traps, when he visits us on occasions. Peter, on the other hand, patrols the property like the homeguard and shoots moles at point-blank range when he sees the earthy heaps erupt or notices worm-seeking birds signalling the moles' four-hourly cycle of activity. Both methods of disposal are quick and effective – if and when the brothers succeed. I have never found that the use of garlic, mothballs, euphorbias or inverted bottles does anything more than cause a possible temporary diversion to the moles' mission in life. The alternative uses of gas or poison are naturally absolutely taboo here; I would rather live with the large brown heaps of soil and at least have the pleasure of watching nearby blackbirds and robins on worm-alert, and laugh at the adrenalin rush which they and the moles combine to give the mole-catchers in my life!

Chemicals are never applied on the Bird Garden lawn, or needed to keep this lawn luxuriously green all year. The white clover manufactures its own natural fertilizer and successfully competes with most other weeds. The result is pleasing for us and creates a healthy environment for birds.

Summary
This area of grass is very easily steered and managed to be a healthy and productive feeding ground for birds. At the same time, it looks very attractive and complements one of my favourite parts of the garden, which Peter and I gaze onto during our many, happy bird-watching hours. The lawn has the conventional appearance that most gardeners seem to look for, but with just that extra wildlife bonus.

The Chalk Bank and Mound

The chalk bank was our initial inspiration; our very latest project (the mound) is inspired by the earlier experience – and one which happened by default – of growing wildflowers on chalk. When our garden was in the early stages of construction we had used a combination of rubble from the council tip and chalk from a local quarry to help build some of the paths. One year a small bank of the chalk was left unused for a summer season. To our surprise, we soon had wildflowers growing in a delicate little colony, including a fuzz of kidney vetch, tall spires of weld and lacy heads of wild carrot. The chalk must have contained a wealth of much-valued local seed which, when exposed to the light, burst into the joy of life. The path had to be diverted around the amazing feature which had 'spontaneously combusted'!

Lessons learned
However, in subsequent years the plant population became increasingly less delicate, and tough grasses and creeping buttercup marched in, displacing the early pioneers. The bank of chalk was less than 40cm (18in) at the highest point and the depth was insufficient to prevent these greedier volunteer plants from invading and benefiting from the rich, dark loam that lay beneath. However, with careful management, including regular pulling and cutting of the grass, digging up creeping buttercups (but allowing meadow buttercups) and adding wildflower plants of my choice, I eventually encouraged the wildflowers to reach a happy alliance.

Our small Chalk Bank was the inspiration for this larger Chalk Mound. We set up our latest project in order to help conserve some of our threatened local downland plants.

Resolving the contest

We planted field scabious and devil's-bit scabious, which enjoyed the conditions we had inadvertently created. Butterflies, bees and other insects greatly favoured these plants, situated as they were in this sheltered, sunny site near my large, round nectar garden. Ladies' bedstraw was planted near the base of the heap and soon made a strong colony of attractive fine-leaved plants that look deceptively innocuous but are, in fact, quite thuggish as they spread into an impenetrable mass in the more fertile soil near the base of the bank.

A mixed bag of arrivals

Ragwort appeared, as ragwort does and, being former farmers and horse-owners, we are more than well aware of the toxic nature of this plant. Ragwort is a pest weed and must on no account be allowed to spread. Conflicting interests have to be resolved because it is a simply wonderful nectar plant. I play with fire and allow a couple of plants asylum but I am 100 per cent scrupulous in cutting off the flowers the very second they start to set seed and prepare themselves to be air-lifted across country, by way of their parachute seed mechanisms. I diligently

remove every other ragwort plant from the property. I once introduced stripy caterpillars of the flamboyant cinnabar moth to discover the effectiveness of a truly biological method of control. They certainly demolished the ragwort, moved onto groundsel, but then apparently left Sticky Wicket when they ran out of food plants. I understood, of course, but I felt a bit abandoned. If we persecute their food plant, we cannot expect to rely on natural predators to help us control such problem weed species, which certainly exist in some grassland. Far less contentious were the meadow crane's-bills, which cleverly seeded themselves from a nearby patch where cowslips also grow willingly. I transferred a few of those cowslips and they self-seed and increase each year. Some very beautiful purple-coloured orchids miraculously appeared a year or so after I had added yellow rattle to suppress the grass growth. They stirred up a great debate among plantsmen, who argued the case for the pyramidal orchid but mostly pronounced them to be a hybrid between the common spotted and marsh orchid. I just gazed upon their beauty and kept silent!

The birth of a new project

I had learned a lot from the chalky squatters but when I compared their growth and behaviour with the local downland plants, I realized I would need a much deeper chalk mound if a permanent and more successful feature were to be made that would give a respite home to a wider range of our beleaguered wildflowers.

Local source of inspiration and seed stocks

I was certainly inspired to try. I was touched by the beauty of the diminishing patches of the local flora that have managed to survive the intensification of farming and the developments and changes to our surrounding countryside. We are lucky to be able to ride along wildflower-lined bridleways which cross chalk hills within a mile of our clay-lined valley. I could quite legally save a few seeds from the wildflowers I had noticed, providing they were taken from species found growing abundantly. I also asked a local farmer for permission to take cuttings and small divots of turf from part of his downland, which he happened to be rather heedlessly carving up to widen his farm track. The plants would otherwise have been interred in the construction work and lost forever.

A small landscaping operation

I chose a sheltered, south-facing site for my new downland plant haven. It is set in a corner of the Davey Meadow, close to part of my native hedgerow, which offers protection and caterpillar food plants to increase my chances of enticing butterflies to visit and hopefully breed. We imported 30 tons of chalk from the original local quarry where the environmental impact of chalk extraction is minimal. The only chalk now removed is the incidental landfall when it needs to be cleared. We moulded our heap into a slight crescent shape to give added protection from 'the wings' and to trap the heat to make the site as warm as possible for butterflies and other insects. As we landscaped the chalk I set in a few chunks of clay, near the base, to give some variety to the harsh and singular conditions we were deliberately creating, thereby generating extra seeding opportunities for certain plant species to get established. I know that cowslips like limy clay so perhaps this will help their establishment. To avoid confrontation with the planning authorities, the height of our giant white 'croissant–like' feature was not to exceed 1.8m (6ft). It measured about 12m (14 yd) from tip to tip of the crescent edges, where the chalk was most shallow, and about 7 m (22ft) across at the widest point. We then trod one or two ledges at an angle of about 45° to the ground – rather as sheep do on the sides of chalk hills. Our purpose was to stabilize the chalk and help prevent erosion of both chalk and seed. I made footholds up the north face so we could reach a sitting place at the top without damaging the special plants on the south side. The surface of the rest of the mound was deliberately left in a variable state with some rough chunks of chalk and some areas of small, pebble-sized pieces so that the seeds would have varied conditions and mini-environments to establish, as they do, for example, when cliffs fall or erode. We deliberately left 'mini-mounds' for small, ground-hugging plants such as thyme, rockrose, harebells and burnet, which are very often found growing on the micro-environment of rocky ridges or on anthills in downland.

Sowing the mound

Towards the end of September the new site was ready to plant and sow. Starting at the top of the mound, I set in the precious divots and the plants I had grown from seed during the previous year. I helped them along using just a little low-grade and exhausted garden compost from old tomato pots. This would be just enough to help

the plants adjust from the luxury of the nursery world to their nutrient-starved and exposed territory. I used a mixture of sand, leaf-mould and the same tired old compost as a carrier for my treasured, hand-gathered, local seeds. These were then sparsely scattered, concentrating on the top of the mound and on the southerly aspect. The northerly slope would be more or less left to regenerate naturally but, to help stabilize the chalk, I sowed seed of some of the pioneering species, such as wild mignonette, weld and wild carrot, and planted a tiny proportion of the divots of sedges and fine-leaved grasses. The only other grass I sowed with the south-aspect mix was quaking grass, with its uniquely trembling flower-heads, and which Peter and I particularly love.

Planting at the base
Near the bottom of the mound I set a few chunks of the ladies' bedstraw, meadow crane's-bills and greater knapweed which I had in store. From my previous experience I was fairly sure the bedstraw would help act as a 'fire-break' between the

A September sowing of locally harvested seed from a nearby sheep-drove. The narrow path is sown with a mixture of fescues and other grasses to provide butterfly habitat.

chalk flora and some of the more rugged plants of the hay meadow that surrounds the mound. Meadow crane's-bills will undoubtedly be happiest where the soil is a little more moist at the base of the mound and may just be competitive enough to share with the bedstraw, especially if I transferred plants of each in the right proportions to benefit the former. The flamboyant greater knapweed will appreciate the alkaline conditions but will also benefit from just a little of the fertility found nearer the base where the chalk is shallow. I intend to make a gentle transition from the flora of the clay to that of the chalk.

My seed selection

My seed mix has been carefully compiled to include a high proportion of the species of wildflowers that I suspect will be the most difficult to establish but I am prepared to be made a monkey of when they perversely turn all my plans around during the shake-up that lies ahead. In the first year of so, I expect there to be a rush of kidney vetch and wild carrot, interspersed with spires of weld and mignonette. I think the glaucous sedge, bird's-foot trefoil, marjoram, selfheal, St John's wort, cat's-ear, goatsbeard, salad burnet, rough hawkweed, autumn hawkbit, burnet saxifrage, cowslips and agrimony will soon get their feet in the door and hopefully some of the field scabious, small scabious and devil's-bit scabious will do so too. Orchids are a law unto themselves, but I will wave a few ripe stems, like magic dust, over the mound and hope the spell is cast. I am not sure how the rockroses, centaury, harebells, and thymes will respond to being introduced to their new environment. I will sow their seeds on the top of the mound and on the mini-mounds to give them an advantage in the contest that will eventually occur.

Project summary

This sort of habitat creation is fairly hit and miss; Mother Nature must stifle a giggle at our gung-ho efforts, however caring, committed or even fanatical we are! I may not be able to recreate the perfect plant and wildlife communities found on ancient downland, but at least I can be confident that I will get a result that will benefit a reasonably wide range of wildlife and help to conserve at least some of our beautiful local wild plants, which are constantly at risk. Of course, it would be comparatively simple just to dump a load of chalk and sprinkle an appropriate packet of commercially produced wildflower seeds. It would be sod's law if results seemed to compare well but I much enjoy the extra detail involved in making the project as exacting as possible. From what I see in the countryside around me and from what I learn from botanists and ecologists with a far superior knowledge, I am totally sold on the ecological bonus of growing local seed and trying to imitate the habitat 'from whence they were delivered'!

A Mini-Meadow on Gravel

I believe anyone can make even a pocket handkerchief-sized meadow in their garden! I have an area that is just a few metres (yards) square and demonstrates how many species of wildflowers and grasses can be grown on a tiny patch. There are about 30 at present: a similar mix of ingredients to the Davey Meadow. The secret, as I have shown, is to establish meadows on poor soil which is starved of nutrients, and there are various ways to try and achieve this ideal state. My mini-meadow is growing on little more than hardcore and gravel, albeit that beneath it lurks the sort of fertile soil that many gardeners would die for! This 'meadowette' flowers for months and is cut once a year in autumn so there is no pain and all gain to be found with this small project.

The story

As with so many of our wildflower experiences, unforeseen circumstances led us to make this little patch, which began as a result of a 'meadow rescue' and includes some of the pieces of turf and seed from our local village meadow which, as I reported earlier, was shamefully ploughed up to make what turned out to be a dysfunctional football pitch. Each of the few survivors has a unique thumbprint and should be treasured and conserved for the local flora and fauna it supports. So, when the digger was hired to rip up the little gem of a village meadow, it was with not even the

The mini-meadow in an odd corner of the garden. We used hardcore and gravel to create the starved soil conditions that our rescued wildflower turf required and very soon we counted over 30 native grassland species growing in an area less than 3 sq m (3½ sq yd).

slightest twinge of conscience that I confiscated two or three barrowloads of turf to take into safe-keeping at Sticky Wicket. Some of the turf was laid in the Davey Meadow and the New Hay Meadow, but I held back a few sods for reasons I can no longer remember. During the winter they began to look settled, laid where they were on our gravelly hard-standing. I decided to make them a bit cosier so I put more path gravel, or 'hogging,' around them and sowed some yellow rattle to check the grass, which was already responding to the soil in the gravel mix. I added just a few extra seeds that I had gathered from the site before it was made desolate. In the space of a couple of years the wildflowers proliferated, set seed and rapidly spread, rippling out into the nearby gravel. I will harvest the seed each year and make sure that a nucleus of that meadow is conserved so that, as a gesture, I can perpetuate those local plants at home and on local projects. I have already returned some of the seed for our village-school meadow project. Perhaps the next generation will eventually learn to value their environment more than we have done? I hope it won't be too late.

Setting the picture

We put a locally crafted wattle fence behind the little triangle of grass to give it a rustic setting and made a window in the wattle through which we can glimpse our vintage tractor – 'the little grey Fergie' – very Chelsea! I sowed blue-tufted vetch and yellow meadow vetchling near the wattle and both are obligingly clambering decoratively upwards. So yet again an unplanned incident has become one of the highlights of a tour of our meadows. Even if I had not had the turf, the way the wildflowers seeded so readily proves I could have probably just sowed seed on top of the path gravel. In hindsight, I think it would have been a good plan to lay a sheet of horticultural fabric beneath the sandy gravel to form a membrane between the plants and the loam that lurks underneath. Plants are clever at seeking sustenance and the more adventurous ones would almost certainly be those least conducive to the wellbeing of a mini-meadow.

Putting the case for knapweed

In a very limited space, I would choose common knapweed above all other meadow plants. It is suitably competitive in grass, visited by masses of nectar-seeking insects and it flowers prettily for almost three months. Even if you need to cut the mini-meadow early in the year – perhaps to clear bulb foliage or restrain the volume of grass – knapweed will obligingly recover and flower just a little later in its season. Some forms of this thistle-like wildflower have 'rayed' outer florets making them look like their more showy, scabious-like and finely foliaged relation, greater knapweed, which is more choosy about growing conditions and prefers chalky soil. It is well worth selecting seed from plants that have interesting forms and colour variations, which can be paler or more intense purples. Very occasionally, they are white, which should appeal to gardeners who are looking for attractive and unusual plants that also have all the merits of helping to attract and support beneficial wildlife.

Food for thought

This project made me think what a simple solution this sort of procedure would be for any one wanting a small, garden-sized meadow and I began to supply one or two 'wannabe' meadow-makers with a 'starter sod' to form the nucleus of their project.

Landscaping in this way would be an expensive method of creating a large meadow but on a small scale, and compared to other garden-making operations, it is a very cheap way of getting a quick, effective and gratifying result. Small as it is, and in spite of all the other grassland projects from which our wildlife can chose, the mini-meadow has its share of visiting creatures, showing just how valuable even a tiny patch of wildlife-friendly grassland can be. Almost anyone could fit a mini-meadow into a corner of their garden – even if not with our particular provenance of snatch and grab!

A final word

Meadow restoration or creation takes time, persistence and patience to achieve heart-warming results. I do hope more and more landowners will be encouraged to discover the pleasures of habitat creation and conservation, whether the available area comprises rolling acres of farmland, a disused pony paddock, a redundant lawn, a small corner of the garden or even a window box! Every little helps.

Remember our traditional meadows were not 'created' – they evolved. We are having to do things back to front to meet the desperate need to conserve our threatened British native flora and create a wildlife habitat. It takes many years for a truly compatible, species-rich plant community to evolve. Nature has to juggle her balancing act while we have to do our best to steer the right course in order to help. I promise that it is worth every minute of our effort and is deeply rewarding. My meadows are breathtakingly beautiful. After 15 years of making my wildlife garden, my most treasured and golden moments are unequivocally those spent in my magical meadows.

The window in the wattle screen allows a glimpse of our Ferguson tractor, 'Little Grey Fergi', parked among a forest of purple loosetrife and teasel seed-heads. They also serve who stand and wait – for hay-making time!

GRASSLAND PLANTS AT STICKY WICKET

THE WILDFLOWERS listed in this section all flower between spring and late summer — the majority in June and July. The flowering heights can vary according to the nature of the soil and the corresponding height of the grass sward but are usually around 60cm (2ft) in a hay meadow and considerably less on chalk. In my brief and personal descriptions I have indicated the plants that are exceptions to these generalizations and I have outlined some other distinguishing features which I find help with identification. I mention where there is an observable inter-relationship with wildlife but my comments only scratch the surface of the vast and fascinating subject of 'flora for fauna'.

In describing grasses I have mentioned the caterpillar food plant of the butterflies most of us are likely to attract. Butterflies are so specific in their needs, and their habitat is becoming so increasingly scarce, that our gardens and meadows are important for the survival of many species.

The Davey meadow, the New Hay Meadow and the Mini-meadow
Common meadow plants are usually the easiest and most reliable to establish in a reasonably wide range of conditions. The following plants are the usual components of most basic, standard commercial seed mixes:

Red campion seems happiest hugging the field margins, but it will sometimes venture into open grassland. This wildflower varies considerably in form and in shades of pink, so I try to sow seed from glamorous specimens, such as this splendid example.

YARROW *Achillea millefolium* A valuable herb for grazing stock and a good source of late-summer nectar for a range of insects. The flat, solid flowerheads are white or occasionally pink and the foliage is finely divided.

COMMON KNAPWEED *Centaurea nigra* A superb, long-flowering nectar plant. Its thistle-like, purple flowers attract many bees, butterflies and other insects, including the burnet moths.

WILD CARROT *Daucus carota* A most intriguing plant, appreciated by many sheltering insects for the unique concave form of both bud and seed-head. In late summer, the exquisite, lacy, umbelliferous flowers are usually white but occasionally pink-tinged. The foliage is finely divided and adds to the overall beauty of this plant, which is particular favourite of the soldier beetle (and the author).

LADIES' BEDSTRAW *Galium verum* Tiny clusters of yellow flowers and small, narrow-leafed foliage combine to give the plant a soft, hazy appearance, which belies its ability to slowly commandeer substantial tracts of fertile meadowland and exclude other plants. On starved chalk it is generally more restrained.

CAT'S-EAR *Hypochaeris radicata* Yellow, dandelion-like flowers on stems that rise from a rosette of wavy-edged leaves. An excellent nectar plant with a long flowering season and a good seed source for birds.

OX-EYE DAISY *Leucanthemum vulgare* Twenty-three species of insect visit this glamorous early colonizer of meadowland. The true British species has a rather ragged edge to the white petals and is not 'oversized' like the foreign imports.

RIBWORT PLANTAIN *Plantago lanceolata* The black dots of flowerheads are very pretty when dusted with pollen in spring, when they appear above the strap-shaped, ribbed leaves. A valuable grazing herb and a good provider of seeds for birds.

MEADOW BUTTERCUP *Ranunculus acris* Taller than, and aesthetically superior to, creeping buttercup and a more sociable team player in a grass sward. The slender, branched stems are topped with flowers varying a little between golden and pale yellow and appearing to float above the spring grass.

YELLOW RATTLE *Rhinanthus minor* An attractive, early-flowering pale yellow, cowslip-like flower. It is semi-parasitic, fixing its roots onto those of adjoining grasses, robbing them of water and minerals. Large, flat seeds rattle in the big, round pods, giving the plant its name.

COMMON SORREL *Rumex acetosa* Vibrant wisps of russet-red light up the early summer meadow. It is an important food plant for the small copper butterfly.

SEE ALSO: selfheal (*Prunella vulgaris*)and bird's-foot trefoil (*Lotus corniculatus*) on page 145 and the following grasses; common bent (*Agrostis capillaris*), crested dog's-tail (*Cynosurus cristatus*) and red fescue (*Festuca rubra*), which are in the Grasses listed on pages 151-3.

These additional, more unusual plants (also in the Davey, New Hay and Mini-Meadows) boost the biodiversity and extend the overall flowering period of wildflowers suitable for neutral loam and clay soil.
* Denotes those plants which particularly like or tolerate damp soil.

*SNEEZEWORT *Achillea ptarmica* A welcome, late-summer addition to the meadow; this plant has flat-topped heads of daisy-type flowers with central florets that are more white than yellow. It has angular stems with narrow, finely toothed leaves.

FRAGRANT AGRIMONY *Agrimonia repens* Has fragrant foliage and yellow flowers on slender spires. The plant is bigger and more branched than *A. eupatoria*.

LADIES' SMOCK *Cardamine pratensis* This is an early-flowering plant of damp meadows with blush-pink flowers. An essential food and nectar plant for the orange-tip butterflies.

*MEADOW THISTLE *Cirsium dissectum* A striking purple-flowered, spineless thistle on a single stem with silvery backed basal leaves.

MARSH THISTLE *Cirsium palustre* Tall and slender with handsome foliage, it is one of the aristocrats of thistles. The small, neat purple flowers are greatly valued by many insects.

PIGNUT *Conopodium majus* Difficult to establish but forms great colonies when conditions are suitable. It has a dense mat of filigree foliage at the base of slender stems of delicate white umbelliferous flowers in early summer.

COMMON SPOTTED ORCHID *Dactylorhiza fuchsii* Spikes of exquisitely marked flowers, which vary in colour between pale, mauve-pink and deeper mauve-purple. As the name suggests, the basal foliage is spotted.

*MEADOWSWEET *Filipendula ulmaria* Fluffy, ivory white flowers, with a sweet scent, attracting many mid- to late-summer insects. Forms strong colonies with tough rootstocks, which can out-compete other plants.

MARSH BEDSTRAW *Galium palustre* Produces a frothy mass of white, deliciously scented flowers on many stems branching from a slim base.

DYERS' GREENWEED *Genista tinctoria* Uncommon in most hay meadows. A semi-woody dye-plant with dark green leaves and handsome, golden-yellow flower spikes.

MEADOW CRANE'S-BILL *Geranium pratense* Bees enjoy the nectar of this glamorous, blue, early-summer-flowering meadow plant. It prefers limestone, but seems quite at home in my neutral loam.

MOUSE-EAR HAWKWEED *Hieracium pilosella* Has pale yellow flowers with a tinge of orange underneath, and hairy leaves and stems. Good nectar plant.

Meadow crane's-bill *Geranium pratense*

GRASS VETCHLING *Lathyrus nissolia* A grass-like plant with extraordinary electric-pink pea flowers appearing to dangle in mid-air! One of the few annuals able to persist in a grass sward.

MEADOW VETCHLING *Lathyrus pratensis* Pretty yellow pea-type flowers on stems which clamber among other grassland plants and hedgerows, from June to September.

AUTUMN HAWKBIT *Leontodon autumnalis* Slender, almost pinnate leaves and branched stems with a dandelion-like flower. Flowering period extends from July to October, providing nectar late into the year.

*RAGGED ROBIN *Lychnis flos-cuculi* Likes ground that is moist for at least part of the year. In June and July it produces a stunning haze of raggedy pink where colonized in our New Hay Meadow.

CORKY-FRUITED WATER DROPWORT *Oenanthe pimpinelloides* Only found in south-west Britain, in particular in Dorset, so it is a plant with important local provenance. It has quite a chunky flower- and seed-head, as umbellifers go, and is relatively low growing. Unlike most dropworts, it is non-toxic to stock.

*COMMON BISTORT *Persicaria bistorta* (syn. *Polygonum bistorta*) The tough rhizomes preclude most other plants in the damp areas where the plant colonizes. Broad, dock-like leaves further smother out other plants. It has pink spikes on single stems in early summer. An attractive plant, it is reputed to have many herbal virtues.

CREEPING TORMENTIL *Potentilla reptans* This tiny, buttercup-like flower secretes nectar to attract pollinating insects in June to September. It has creeping, rooting stems with dark green, strawberry-like foliage.

*FLEABANE *Pulicaria dysenterica* Yellow, button-centred, daisy-flowers provide late-summer nectar for many insects, particularly the small copper butterfly. Vigorous root stock allows the plant to spread competitively through the grass sward.

Great burnet (*Sanguisorba officinalis*)

*BURNET, GREAT *Sanguisorba officinalis* A tall plant with deep maroon oval seed-heads which glow at the tips of branched flowerheads adorning the late summer meadow. Grows well in damp conditions, tolerating dense clay.

SAWWORT *Serratula tinctoria* Like a 'tidy' miniature knapweed, it is late-flowering with conspicuous, starry, tan seed-heads in autumn.

*PEPPER SAXIFRAGE *Silaum silaus* Often an indicator of ancient meadows and can be difficult to establish. Pale yellow umbelliferous flowers give this lovely plant a sophisticated appearance.

*BETONY *Stachys officinalis* Purple flowers on erect stems punctuate the grass sward in August and September. A valuable late nectar plant, popular with the burnet moth.

LESSER STITCHWORT *Stellaria graminea* Has tiny, starry white flowers as beautiful as they are inconspicuous at the base of the early summer grass sward.

DEVIL'S-BIT SCABIOUS *Succisa pratensis* Has small, blue, pinhead-cushion flowers on branched stems, providing nectar-rich platforms for butterflies in late summer. Surprisingly, this plant is as happy in damp clay as it is in dry chalky conditions, such as downland. The marsh fritillary butterfly will lay its eggs only on this particular plant.

GOAT'S-BEARD *Tragopogon pratensis* The yellow flowers of 'Jack-go-to-bed-at-noon' open very early in the morning and close around mid-day. The fruiting head is even larger and more spectacular than a dandelion 'clock'. It has bluish-green, grass-like leaves which clasp the medium-tall stems.

*TUFTED VETCH *Vicia cracca* Elegant blue rows of pea-type flowers can be seen between June and August, held on fine-leaved foliage. Sprawls among and over other plants, forming dense clumps and attracting insects.

COMMON VETCH *Vicia sativa* ssp *nigra* A favourite with certain bumblebees, attracted to its pretty bright pink flowers early in the summer season.

See also: bugle (*Ajuga*), dandelion (*Taraxacum*) and medick (*Medicago*) (under Flowering Lawn on page 144) and other grasses in the Grasses list on pages 151-3.

Goat's-beard (*Tragopogon pratensis*)

UNWANTED (OR VIEWED WITH MIXED FEELINGS)
CREEPING BUTTERCUP *Ranunculus repens* This plant spreads rapidly with an insistent, creeping root system which, like white clover, smothers out other plants.

RED CLOVER *Trifolium pratense* While certainly useful to some bumblebees, legumes such as this, with their nitrogen fixing attributes, can be instrumental in increasing the soil fertility (and therefore unwanted).

WHITE CLOVER *Trifolium repens* The same applies to this plant, which presents additional problems in aggressive occupation of territory (See also Flowering Lawn).

WET, ROUGH CORNER OF THE DAVEY MEADOW
The plants in this damp and extremely fertile area are generally tall, vigorous and competitive growers. There are some that may be perceived to be lacking in aesthetic appeal and with certain 'anti-social' characteristics, but they are deliberately included because of their great benefit to the wildlife which visits our grassland.

WILD ANGELICA *Angelica sylvestris* Tall, umbelliferous plant with smooth, stylish stems and foliage. Its elegant, late-summer flowers are usually white but sometimes pale pink.

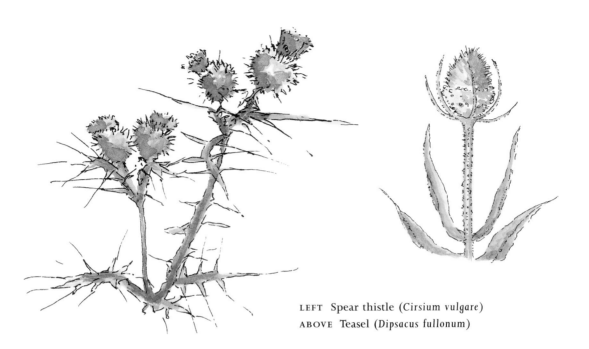

LEFT Spear thistle (*Cirsium vulgare*)
ABOVE Teasel (*Dipsacus fullonum*)

GREAT BURDOCK *Arctium lappa* Has large, leathery leaves at the base of branched stems with nectar-rich, thistle-like flowers. Familiar, barbed burrs ensure widespread dispersal via the passing fauna on which they hitch a lift.

CREEPING THISTLE *Cirsium arvense* This plant is generally unpopular enough to be on DEFRA's proscribed list. Nevertheless, to the painted lady butterfly it is one of its essential plants and to me its neat mauve flowers have a wonderful, warm, quintessentially summery scent.

SPEAR THISTLE *Cirsium vulgare* An architectural and very prickly plant, which is also wonderfully nectar-rich. The large mauve flowers are a special favourite with bumblebees, and goldfinches feast on the seeds at the base of the silvery-white thistledown.

TEASEL *Dipsacus fullonum* Architectural plant with large, thistle-like, nectar-rich flowers. The tall, stout, prickly stems have around them cup-shaped structures collecting rain water. A valuable seed source for goldfinches throughout the winter.

GREAT WILLOW-HERB *Epilobium hirsutum* This tall, showy, purple-pink willow-herb is sometimes called 'codlins and cream.' Like other willow-herbs, it is a food plant for the spectacular elephant hawk-month. It forms dense clumps with a virulent root system.

HEMP AGRIMONY *Eupatorium cannabinum* Tall, clump-forming plant with flat heads of fluffy, dusky pink flowers between July and September. One of the most popular and well-visited nectar plants I know.

HOGWEED *Heracleum sphondylium* The boldest of umbelliferous plants with large, hairy leaves and strong stems with white or occasionally pinkish flowers, attracting many insects.

YELLOW FLAG *Iris pseudacorus* Has striking sword-like leaves with showy bright yellow, early summer flowers pollinated by bees.

*GIPSYWORT *Lycopus europaeus* The toothed leaves on the tall stems are a more distinguishing feature than the inconspicuous pale-pink clusters of flowers around the base of each pair of leaves.

PURPLE LOOSESTRIFE *Lythrum salicaria* Tall, stately spires of magenta-pink flowers attract bees and butterflies. Their stiff stems hold long-standing seed-heads with a copious seed supply for birds.

GREAT PLANTAIN *Plantago major* A broad-leaved plant with spiked flowerheads, producing bountiful seeds for birds. It tends to grow where the ground has been trampled by stock or in wheel ruts.

CURLED DOCK *Rumex crispus* A more slender and elegant version of the dock discussed below.

BROAD-LEAVED DOCK *Rumex obtusifolius* This plant has large, unattractive leaves but is redeemed by its ability to support many beetles and moths. It has thick flowerheads which can sometimes be surprisingly attractive and are seed-laden for birds.

Nettle *Urtica dioica*

COMMON FIGWORT *Scrophularia nodosa* An upright plant with hairless, square stems rising from knobbly rhizomes. Sunlight highlights the glowing flecks of tiny red flowers which wasps and hoverflies find irresistible.

HOARY RAGWORT *Senecio erucifolius* Claimed by some to be an atypically non-toxic ragwort, but not all experts agree. It is a much-valued nectar source, but it would be prudent to prevent it from setting seed and spreading out of bounds or onto neighbouring property.

COMFREY *Symphytum officinale* A large, coarse-leaved plant with tough tap-roots. The flowering season begins in early spring and continues through the summer with pink, white, blue or purple flowers that are adored by bees.

NETTLE *Urtica dioica* Simply one of the most important food plants for a range of butterflies and other insects. An indicator of fertile ground.

COMMON VALERIAN *Valeriana officinalis* Enjoys variable conditions but thrives in moist soil. Good early nectar plant with blush-pink flowers on tall stems in May and June.

GRASSES AND RUSHES INCLUDE: Tufted hair grass (*Deschampsia cespitosa*), hard rush (*Juncus inflexus*), soft rush (*J. effusus*), greater pond sedge (*Carex riparia*) and others (see Grasses listed on pages 151-3).

UNWANTED PLANTS
HEMLOCK WATER DROPWORT *Oenanthe crocata* Another tall white umbelliferous plant which is very stout-looking. This one is highly toxic and needs to be carefully identified and controlled to prevent it spreading and causing harm.

Garlic mustard *Alliaria petiolata*

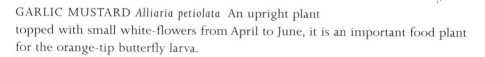

COMMON RAGWORT *Senecio jacobaea* Well-known yellow flowerheads on strong, medium height stems. It is illegal to allow common ragwort to spread onto neighbouring land because it is poisonous to stock.

SOME WILDLIFE-FRIENDLY GRASSLAND PLANTS FOUND IN FIELD EDGES AND HEDGEROWS
From the extensive range of bank and hedgerow plants, I have selected a few which are special for wildlife and tend to grow in the fruitful zone where plants of sheltered hedgerow and open grassland merge.

GARLIC MUSTARD *Alliaria petiolata* An upright plant topped with small white-flowers from April to June, it is an important food plant for the orange-tip butterfly larva.

COW PARSLEY *Anthriscus sylvestris* The earliest of the umbelliferous plants, providing an ample nectar supply for emerging insects. It seldom spreads into open grassland, usually confining itself to the slightly shaded conditions in field margins.

HEMP AGRIMONY *Eupatorium cannabinum* Tall, clump-forming plant with flat heads of fluffy, dusky pink flowers between July and September. One of the most popular and well-visited nectar plants I know.

HEDGE BEDSTRAW *Galium mollugo* Clouds of tiny white flowers billow outwards from the hedge base from June to September.

SQUARE-STEMMED ST JOHN'S-WORT *Hypericum tetrapterum* Clusters of tiny yellow flowers are especially enticing to hoverflies from June to September.

WHITE DEADNETTLE *Lamium album* A gracious-looking plant with a vigorous root system, making it better able to compete in grassland than its red relative, with which it shares its worthy, nectar-producing qualities.

RED DEADNETTLE *Lamium purpureum* This short, pink-flowered plant will only survive where the grass is short but, from March to August, it offers an excellent nectar source for bumblebees.

MUSK MALLOW *Malva moschata* Finely dissected leaves and large, showy, pink summer flowers make this one of the grassland stars.

PRIMROSE *Primula vulgaris* The beautiful, pale yellow flowers provide a valuable source of nectar for the brimstone butterfly in spring.

RED CAMPION *Silene dioica* Moths are attracted to the flowers that vary in colour from deep rose to pale pink. A delightful plant preferring field edges.

WHITE CAMPION *Silene pratensis* Less common than red campion, occurring mainly where ground is disturbed. A beautiful plant, which is also valued by moths.

HEDGE WOUNDWORT *Stachys sylvatica* The magenta flowers are, on close inspection, quite attractive. Flowering from July to September, it is especially important for the survival of certain bumblebees.

SEE ALSO: tufted vetch (*Vicia cracca*), common vetch (*V. sativa ssp. nigra*), meadow vetchling (*Lathyrus pratensis*) and meadow grasses, especially cocksfoot (*Dactylis glomerata*) and Yorkshire fog (*Holcus lanata*) in Grasses listed on pages 151-3.

The Frog Garden lawn
I have chosen wildlife-attracting plants that can adapt their mode of growth and can thereby withstand a fairly regular (but carefully judged) mowing regime.
* Plants appreciating wetter areas

*BUGLE *Ajuga reptans* Low creeping plant colonizing damp meadow areas. It has short blue flower spikes providing early nectar for bees.

DAISY *Bellis perennis* Plants form a close mat, thriving in short mown grass and annoying many traditional gardeners! A perfect component of the flowering lawn.

GROUND-IVY *Glechoma hederacea* The creeping and rooting habit of this plant allows it to colonize patches of grass. The spring flowers are in whorls and the colour varies from pinkish-mauve to purple. In some cases bronze foliage helps to heighten the depth of the darker tones.

LESSER HAWKBIT *Leontodon taraxacoides* Short, slender stems with solitary yellow, dandelion-like flowerheads rise from basal rosettes of wavy leaves.

BIRD'S-FOOT TREFOIL *Lotus corniculatus* The height of the plant can vary to match the growing conditions and the way it is managed. The yellow, pea-type flowers can be produced at ground level or on a medium-height plant that offers nectar and an essential food plant for the common blue butterfly and is extremely important to a wide range of other insects, including certain skippers.

BLACK MEDICK *Medicago lupulina* As with red clover, medick can increase the soil fertility, but this pretty little yellow-flowered plant is beneficial for butterflies.

*SILVERWEED *Potentilla anserina* Flowering stems are creeping and rooting, with clear yellow buttercup-like flowers from July to August. The name reflects the silky, silvery, pinnate leaves which also make it an attractive member of the community of flowering lawn plants.

SELFHEAL *Prunella vulgaris* A versatile plant that can flower at various heights from 1-45cm (½-18in), depending on its management. Provides nectar over a long flowering period and toleres a wide range of conditions.

LESSER CELANDINE *Ranunculus ficaria* A low-growing plant with gleaming yellow flowers and shining, mottled foliage which studs the lawn in spring. Can be a menace in the garden but is usually fairly innocuous in grassland.

SHEEP'S SORREL *Rumex acetosa* A miniature version of common sorrel with the same russet-red flowers but having a longer-stalked leaf like a barbed spearhead. Said to prefer acid soils, but seems to accept neutral if well-drained soil. I like to grow it to supplement the sorrel-only diet of the small copper butterfly.

DANDELION *Taraxacum officinale* This common plant with its large yellow flowers eclipses all other plants with nectar-bearing virtues. Often persecuted by gardeners, it can cleverly adapt its flowering height to survive in mown grass.

WHITE CLOVER *Trifolium repens* This white-flowered nectar plant has an invasive root system, forming a tight ground-hugging carpet. In lawns, it has the added benefit of increasing soil fertility.

GERMANDER SPEEDWELL *Veronica chamaedrys* Has dainty blue flowers on short creeping stems. It can flower from March to August, but is at its best in spring.

SLENDER SPEEDWELL *Veronica filiformis* More slender stems with smaller leaves and flowers than germander speedwell, but just as pretty.

GRASSES INCLUDE: red fescue (*Festuca rubra*), sheep's fescue (*F. ovina*), rough meadow grass and common bent (*Agrostis capillaris*) in Grasses listed on page 151-3.)

The Chalk Bank and Mound
There is a wealth of plants that flourish on chalk, but I have noted only those that I have found growing near local by-ways rather than including rarities which are outside the remit of a garden project. Sometimes it is the calcareous nature of the soil that is the key to plant survival, but good-drainage and low-nutrient factors make the chalky environment attractive to such a wide range of appealing plants.
* Denotes plants for top of bank where the soil is most nutrient-starved and dry.

AGRIMONY *Agrimonia eupatoria* Medium-height, slender spires with small yellow flowers. A plant believed to have great herbal magical, medicinal and dye properties. Hooked seeds are distributed by people and animals.

KIDNEY VETCH *Anthyllis vulneraria* Kidney-shaped flowerheads composed of yellow flowers, which fade to brown before appearing silvery when in seed. Although the flowers are rich in nectar, it takes a strong insect, such as a bumblebee, to force access. The small blue butterfly will nectar on this and other vetches, but depends on this plant as its sole caterpillar food plant.

*HAREBELL *Campanula rotundifolia* The charismatic, light blue flowers dance on the finest of wiry stems. The creeping underground stems produce basal clusters of heart-shaped leaves on long stalks. The flowering stems have leaves which, by contrast, are more grass-like.

COMMON CENTAURY *Centaureum erythraea* Pretty, five-petalled, pink flowers on closely branched stems with pairs of elliptical leaves. This sweet wildflower can vary in height and form to adapt to a range of habitat, but it prefers dry ground.

GREATER KNAPWEED *Centaurea scabiosa* This plant is scabious-like with larger and shaggier flowerheads than common knapweed and with erratic sized, more divided foliage. It is top of the range as a nectar plant and a great beauty.

DWARF THISTLE *Cirsium acaule* The stems are so short they barely exist and the large flowers sit in a rosette of typically prickly but stylish thistle foliage. From July to August up to four flowers will huddle together attracting insects to their level.

CROWN VETCH *Coronilla varia* Round heads of eye-catching, pink, pea-like flowers are held on stems which sprawl or clamber around. An introduced plant but I have included it as I found it naturalized locally.

EYEBRIGHT *Euphrasia nemorosa* This is also a semi-parasite which has sturdy, upright stems with small, white, yellow-centred flowers. The leaves are dark and occasionally purplish-green.

DROPWORT *Filipendula vulgaris* Has fluffy white flowers, like its relative meadowsweet, but with pinkish buds. The foliage is attractively fern-like.

WILD STRAWBERRY *Fragaria vesca* A favourite caterpillar food plant of the grizzled skipper. Although this butterfly requires more specialized habitat than I can offer, I grow this neat little plant 'just in case'!

*COMON ROCKROSE *Helianthemum chamaecistus* Although this low-growing plant has no scent and lacks nectar, it produces an abundance of pollen which insects gather. From June to September the yellow flowers open in the sun, displaying their pretty round flowers, which are generally buttercup-coloured.

*HORSESHOE VETCH *Hippocrepis comosa* This striking plant spreads itself like a yellow mat with its trailing fronds of foliage, which have many leaflets either side of a long leaf stalk. The bonny golden flowers are sometimes red-striped and the seed pods have horseshoe-shaped segments which give the plant its common name. The plant is pollinated by bumblebees and honey bees. (The chalkhill and Adonis butterflies lay their eggs solely on this low-growing plant.)

PERFORATE ST JOHN'S-WORT *Hypericum perforatum* Two narrow wings on the stem distinguish this species from its similar, square-stemmed relative. The growth is very upright, with strong stems supporting multiples of small, long-flowering, yellow flowers which require careful scrutiny to appreciate their wonderful botanical detail. The russet-coloured seed-heads are also subtly pleasing.

FIELD SCABIOUS *Knautia avensis* Has prolific growth of stems that are usually branched and has divided leaves which form the diet of caterpillars of certain field- edge moths, which are one of the most memorable sights in the late-summer meadow.

FAIRY FLAX *Linum catharticum* The upright slender stems are just a few centimetres (inches) high with minute, starry, white flowers on a loosely branched flowerhead from June to September. The small, narrow leaves have one central vein. The whole plant is remarkably dainty but highly inconspicuous.

ROUGH HAWKBIT *Leontodon hispidus* Dandelion-like flowers on single hairy stems with broad, wavy-edged leaves; a good nectar provider from June to September.

RED BARTSIA *Odonites verna* Like yellow rattle, this plant has the ability to live on grasses as a semi-parasite and is similarly short in height. The flowers are pink and the foliage has a covering of fine white hairs, which gives this plant a dusty appearance.

REST-HARROW *Ononis repens* So called because its matted stems and deep roots were said to thwart the efficiency of horse-drawn cultivating equipment. Attractive, pink pea-flowers bloom along the length of this low-growing plant's trailing stems.

WILD MARJORAM Origanum vulgare A highly
aromatic plant which many butterflies,
especially meadow browns and gatekeepers,
find totally irresistible. Clusters of pink flowers
fan out on branched stems. Sometimes
purplish bracts heighten the depth of the
flower colour.

BURNET SAXIFRAGE Pimpinella saxifrage
Another white-flowered, umbelliferous plant;
this one is delicate-looking and flowers from
July to August.

HOARY PLANTAIN Plantago media This most
elegant of plantains appears to have a pale pink
aura when pollen-laden between May and

Cowslip Primula veris

August. The flowers have a delicate scent which attracts numerous bees. The stalks
radiate from flat rosettes of broad, deeply veined, oval leaves.

COMMON MILKWORT Polygala vulgaris A strange little flower worthy of close
scrutiny. Its petals appear to be 'encapsulated' by two of its sepals, which are the
same colour. That colour may be white, pink, mauve or blue, and the flowers are
on short spikes. It has alternate leaves up the short, upright stems.

COWSLIP Primula veris This is spring-flowering, the colour varying from
primrose yellow to yellowy-orange. The delicately perfumed flowers are visited by
long-tongued insects such as moths and bees. Cowslips survive best in an open
sward where the grasses are not too overwhelming.

BULBOUS BUTTERCUP Ranunculus bulbosa The earliest-flowering buttercup,
having taller and slightly paler flowers than creeping buttercup and with a far less
belligerent nature. The base of the stem is swollen and each leaf has a stalked
middle lobe, helping to distinguish it from other buttercups.

WELD Reseda luteola This is a tall plant compared with most of my chalk lovers
and towers above the others in an imperial way with pale, limy-yellow flowers on

elegant spikes. (It was an important dye plant, yielding yellow pigment used by dyers from the medieval period onwards). Interestingly, it has heliotropic flowers which face east in the morning and west by tea-time.

SALAD BURNET *Sanguisorba minor*   From June to September round, brownish-red flowerheads bob at the top of short, upright stems. The leaves are composed of paired rows of toothed leaflets, giving the plant a distinguished appearance.

SMALL SCABIOUS *Scabiosa columbaria*   More diminutive in both flower and foliage, this plant is just as beguiling as its more robust relative and shares the ability to attract a mass of insects, including many butterflies.

*WILD THYME *Thymus praecox*   A delightfully aromatic plant with a prostrate habit and needing a very thin grass sward in which to spread. In fact, a hummock, such as an ant-hill, gives the plant an advantage in this respect. (Gardeners can only dream of encountering the very special large blue butterfly, which depends on this plant for its very survival, but many bees and butterflies favour the plant for its nectar.)

VERVAIN *Verbena officinalis*   Such a 'will 'o the wisp' sort of plant should look good and be at home on my chalk. Its spiky, pronged stems bear the tiniest of lilac-coloured flowers at the tip.

GRASSES INCLUDE: Quaking grass (*Briza media*), yellow oat grass (*Trisetum flavescens*), sheep's fescue (*Festuca ovina*) and also glaucous sedge (*Carex flacca*) – see list of grasses below.

Grasses, Sedges and Rushes

I have selected some of the most beautiful and wildlife-friendly of wild meadow grasses and one or two of the many native sedges and rushes. In my list of flowering plants, I have noted some particularly appropriate places for the types of plant, bearing in mind the fragile or robust nature of the floral community for which they form the base. I have stated their significance to butterflies and mentioned the grazing or hay-making value of the relevant grasses.

The following grasses thrive in a variety of conditions and provide a sound base for most meadow seed mixes:

COMMON BENT *Agrostis capillaris* Has loose, open panicles with whorls of much divided branches with a brown or purplish appearance. The short rhizomes make it a good lawn grass. Like other bents, it is a food plant for the gatekeeper, marbled white, meadow brown and small heath butterflies.

SWEET VERNAL *Anthoxanthum odoratum* The grass that emits the breathtaking scent of new-mown hay. It is one of the first meadow grasses to flower and one of the shortest in height, having a fairly short, spiky flowerhead.

CRESTED DOG'S-TAIL *Cynosurus cristatus* One of the most beautiful grasses, especially when back-lit. The flowers-heads are neat, braided-looking, elegant spikes. It is leafy only at the base and has a wiry stem, making it economical with space and an ideal constituent of an assorted floral community.

OTHER MEADOW GRASSES, MANY OF WHICH ARE VALUABLE FOR GRAZING, HAY-MAKING AND WILDLIFE

CREEPING BENT *Agrostis stolonifera* Far prettier than it sounds! The young flowerheads look like slender, dark pencils before opening up to become delicate, airy-fairy and pinkish in mid- to late summer. Creeping, rooting stems are a bit assertive in a young meadow, but this grass has good grazing value.

MEADOW FOXTAIL *Alopecurus pratensis* Early flowering, looking similar to Timothy, but with softer, cylindrical flowerheads on tall stems that yield more to the wind. A good, broad-leaved, early-season grazing grass that thrives in damp meadows.

QUAKING GRASS *Briza media* Triangular purplish-green flowerheads dangle from fine, hairless stalks. The plant appears to tremble or shiver, and when the wind blows, it rattles. Uniquely beautiful, it is a real primadona among grasses, although with so little foliage, it does not signify as fodder for stock. It will grow on chalk or in clay.

GLAUCOUS SEDGE *Carex flacca* Stems and undersides of leaves are bluish-green. Usually has two or three, upright or nodding, purplish-brown flowerheads on each short stem. Likes dry, chalky grassland but equally at home in damp clay. The rhizomatous stems are useful in stabilizing soil and helping prevent erosion.

GREATER POND SEDGE *Carex riparia* This plant forms dense stands in boggy areas. It has upright growth with tall, sharply triangular stems and broad, bluish leaves which are sharp-edged. The handsome, dark, brownish-green flowerheads are long, pointed and cylindrical, making this plant a show-stopper!

COCKSFOOT *Dactylis glomerata* A distinctive grass with dense flowering heads said to resemble the foot of a cockerel. It is a densely tufted grass with coarse foliage, which is greyish-green. A valuable pasture and grazing grass which provides a breeding ground for the Essex and large skipper, ringlet, wall and speckled wood butterflies.

TUFTED HAIR GRASS *Deschampsia cespitosa* Found in abundance in moist places, often indicating ill-drained land. A tussock-forming grass with stunning, translucent, silvery flowerheads on tall, stiff golden stems. Wide, stiff, dark green leaves are refused by horses and usually avoided by cattle. Field mice and insects find it a cosy habitat and it is the breeding place for the grayling butterfly.

SHEEP'S FESCUE *Festuca ovina* Thrives on poor soil, providing sweet grazing for hill sheep. Densely tufted with stiff, upright stems and fine hair-like, tightly rolled leaves. Short, dense panicles with pretty, greyish, violet-tinged flowers which tend to turn one way. It makes a fine, compact lawn grass.

MEADOW FESCUE *Festuca pratensis* A grass found in damp hay-meadows, it has tall stems with delicate, loose panicles with rough, paired branches and the whole, rather heavy flowerhead often bends to one side. The nutritious, tufted foliage is a favourite with cattle and horses.

RED FESCUE *Festuca rubra* The airy inflorescence is sometimes red-tinged. Has fine, thread-like leaves. Can adapt to varied conditions and is both a valuable pasture and lawn grass, and useful to certain grass-dependent butterflies.

YORKSHIRE FOG *Holcus lanata* The stems and the broadish leaves are soft, grey-downy and dew-holding. Its beautiful soft panicles are usually a delicate pinkish-green, deepening to purple and fading to a pale buff, but sometimes the flowers can be a startlingly pale creamy colour. Tolerates a wide range of conditions, wet or dry. It is undeniably beautiful but much too over-powering in a young meadow and can also invade mature grassland to the exclusion of other species. Food plant for the small skipper, speckled wood and wall butterflies

SOFT RUSH *Juncus effusus* On wet ground, this rush forms densely matted circular tufts. It has smooth, leafless, pale green, cylindrical stems containing continuous white pith. The form of the flowers can vary from loosely-branched to globular panicles of greenish-brown.

HARD RUSH *Juncus inflexus* This plant indicates grassland with poor drainage. The stems are tough, dull grey-green, naked and striated, enclosed by purplish sheaths at the base. The pith is not continuous through the stems. It has much-branched panicles of large, erect greenish brown flowers. Said to be poisonous to livestock.

FIELD WOODRUSH *Luzula campestris* This low-growing sedge is conspicuous in spring with its heads of dark copper-brown flowers and brightly contrasting yellow anthers. The margins of the broad, tapering leaves are very hairy.

TIMOTHY *Phleum pratense* A tough, clay-tolerant, excellent fodder grass with dense, prominent, cylindrical flowerheads. There are agricultural varieties that look a bit loutish but the wild ones contribute subtle highlights to the meadow tapestry.

SMALL TIMOTHY *Phleum pratense* ssp *bertolonii* Similar to Timothy grass but generally smaller and less robust.

SMOOTH MEADOW GRASS *Poa pratensis* Rhizomatous grass as useful for grazing as it is hard-wearing for lawns. It has smooth stems and flowerheads similar to, but duller coloured and earlier flowering than, rough meadow grass.

ROUGH MEADOW GRASS *Poa trivialis* A graceful, slender, bright green species having broad tapering leaves and rough stems, all providing nutritious herbage and breeding places for some grass-dependent butterflies. Its creeping rootstock makes it a capable lawn grass even in moist situations. It is also pollution tolerant.

YELLOW OAT GRASS *Trisetum flavescens* A stoloniferous grass with downy leaves and sheaths palatable to livestock. Graceful, early summer flowerheads are shiny yellow. Likes calcareous soil and is tolerant of poor conditions.

MEADOW-GRASS AND WILDFLOWER SEEDS

Carefully source and acquire appropriate seed
Be sure to buy hay-meadow-grasses and wildflower seeds from a reputable seed company (see page 157). It is essential that your seeds come from British native wildflower stock. It is an extra bonus to wildlife if you can go a step further and acquire seed of local provenance. It is illegal to dig up plants in the wild but responsible seed collection is permitted for plants that are not rare, endangered or on private land.

Include yellow rattle to help reduce the competition from grasses
Rattle seed must be sown fresh. Remember, this useful, semi-parasitic, annual plant would be eliminated from grassland if cutting or grazing prevented the formation and spread of the seed for the following year.

Cornfield annuals can be useful and will give you a colourful start
Cornfield annuals will flower only in the first year but, acting as a nurse crop, they will protect the perennial seedlings and help reduce soil erosion. Because they naturally evolved on land that was cultivated for crops, such as cereals, they really only thrive on fertile soils. Once you have reduced the fertility for grassland wildflowers, you will not see the full, colourful impact that these plants have in their accepted environment.

Carefully calibrate the amount of seed required per square metre (yard)
Do not be tempted to overdo the seed rates of cornflower annuals or they may out-compete the young grassland wildflowers. Seedlings are more vulnerable to pest and disease if overcrowded. It

may be wise to err on the side of caution and sow at a rate slightly lower than recommended one.

A special note
I have been extraordinarily fortunate in finding a genuine source of local seed. Few would be so lucky, but it certainly pays to be choosy. Some seed companies are selling seed that is not necessarily harvested from British stock, let alone with a reliable county or regional provenance. Some of our native wildlife are most specific about the plants upon which they feed and breed, and the European stock is not always suitable – most frustrating for the poor creatures when they come so near to, yet so far from, finding an oasis of much-needed habitat. The following is a quote from an English Nature and Wildlife Trust's directive: 'Introduction of non-native species can alter the plant composition of UK habitats and change the gene pool of native species'. (Heaven knows what havoc will be reaped when GM plants inevitably escape or are released.) Fortunately, there are organizations to offer guidance and there are certain seed companies which are extremely conscientious as to seed sourcing, certification and supply (see page 157).

What is on offer from the seed companies
WILD-MEADOW MIXTURES
There are some prime ancient meadow sites (such as Cricklade and Pixie meads) which are regularly harvested for seed and these are commercially available. You can choose a wild-meadow mixture from a site that is compatible with your land, knowing that the seed will have come from genuine British native stock. The species selection can be matched to your soil type but, unless you

happen to live near that harvested meadow, they will not have that special local provenance. It is advisable to check out the species content to see if the mixture contains the ones you wish to include (or even exclude!) and, if so, in what proportions. For instance, I know there is one meadow mix containing a high proportion of Yorkshire fog, which I would be very reluctant to introduce, at least in the early stages of meadow establishment. I just hope the repeated harvesting of these unique heritage sites will not turn out to be detrimental to either the flora or the fauna of the meadows.

MIXTURES FOR SPECIFIC CONDITIONS

You can buy seed mixtures containing species that have been selected and blended by the seed companies. They prepare 'recipes' for every kind of situation – loam, clay, chalk, sand or wetland, and so on. Some companies helpfully state the percentage of each species contained in the mixture. The number of different species is usually quite limited and the selection may vary from supplier to supplier.

GENERAL PURPOSE MIXTURES

There are also 'general purpose' mixtures which contain species that are tolerant of a range of situations. The cost of seed is relative to the number of species of wildflowers and grasses. It is also affected by the ratio of wildflower seed to grass seed – the higher the wildflower proportion the more expensive it is. (The normal ratio is 80:20 per cent grasses to wildflowers.)

MIX AND MATCH

If the mixtures are not exact enough for your project, you can look at the third option, which is to buy the species in individual packets and mix the seed to your own requirements. By careful selection, it is possible to get a mixture of seed appropriate for your land and your objectives.

There are some seed companies that offer a site-specific advisory service, which would be useful to anyone wishing to pursue the subject in depth. I am only just beginning to appreciate how complex the subject can be.

A FEASIBLE COMPROMISE

For the amateur meadow maker, working on domestic projects, I think a suitable compromise can be reached. It is possible to buy a suitable (economical) 'general purpose' mix (from a recommended supplier) and then mix in extra seeds of your choice. You could add your own locally gathered seed or add extra quantities of commercial packets of individual species of seed. In so doing, you can boost the wildflower-to-grass ratio, making it more wildflower rich. If you buy from a seed company which states the county or region of origin of their seed, you can select species of local origin to enhance your ingredients and your ultimate result. It is also possible to focus, for instance, on increasing the proportion of butterfly plants or whatever may be your area of special interest. If you are going to the trouble of preparing and reseeding a site, it is well worth doing some research to make the foundation of your meadow flora as appropriate as possible.

SPECIAL PLANTS

It is fascinating that some plants are so versatile while others need highly specific, often extreme, conditions to survive. In most cases, it is best to avoid 'temperamental' rare species, which usually require special environmental conditions and management requirements. Failed attempts are a sad waste of precious seed. You need to have special knowledge or take expert advice with certain plant species.

Basic meadow plants available as seed
(see list of suppliers opposite)
*Denotes good butterfly plant

BASIC MEADOW WILDFLOWERS
Achillea millefolium Yarrow
Centaurea nigra Common knapweed
Centaurea scabiosa Greater knapweed
Daucus carrota Wild carrot
Galium verum Ladies' bedstraw
Knautia avensis Field scabious
Leucanthemum vulgare Ox-eye daisy
Lotus corniculatus Bird's-foot trefoil
Malva moschata Musk mallow
Plantago lanceolata Ribwort plantain
Plantago media Hoary plantain
Primula veris Cowslip
Prunella vulgaris Selfheal
Ranunculus acris Meadow buttercup
Rhinanthus minor Yellow rattle
Rumex acetosa Common sorrel
Sanguisorba minor Salad burnet
Silene dioica Red campion
Silene latifolia White campion
Vicia sativa ssp nigra Common vetch

Grasses
Agrostis capillaris Common bent
Cynosurus cristatus Crested dog's-tail
Festuca rubra ssp commutata Red fescue
Festuca rubra ssp juncea Red fescue

SPECIAL TO CALCEROUS SOILS
Anthyllis vulneraria Kidney vetch
Filipendula vulgaris Dropwort
Leontodon hispidus Rough hawkbit
Origanum vulgare Wild marjoram
Pimpinella saxifraga Burnet saxifrage
Reseda lutea Wild mignonette

Grasses
Briza media Quaking grass

Cynosurus cristatus Crested dog's-tail
Festuca ovina Sheep's fescue
Festuca rubra ssp juncea Red fescue
Koeleria macrantha Crested hair-grass
Phleum bertolonii Small Timothy
Trisetum flavescens Yellow oat-grass

SPECIAL TO SANDY SOILS
Echium vulgare Viper's bugloss
Linaria vulgaris Common toadflax
Ranunculus bulbosus Bulbous buttercup
Silene vulgaris Bladder campion

Grasses
Agrostis capillaris Common bent
Anthoxanthum odoratum Sweet vernal grass
Cynosurus cristatus Crested dog's-tail
Deschampsia flexuosa Wavy hair-grass
Festuca filiformis Fine-leaved sheep's fescue
Festuca ovina Sheep's fescue
Festuca rubra ssp juncea Red fescue
Phleum bertolonii Small Timothy

SPECIAL TO WET SOILS
Filipendula ulmaria Meadowsweet
Lychnis flos-cuculi Ragged Robin
Silaum silaus Pepper saxifrage
Succisa pratensis Devil's-bit scabious
Cardamine pratensis Ladies' smock

Grasses
Agrostis capillaris Common bent
Alopecurus pratensis Meadow foxtail
Anthoxanthum odoratum Sweet vernal grass
Briza media Quaking grass
Cynosurus cristatus Crested dog's-tail
Deschampsia cespitosa Tufted hair-grass
Festuca rubra ssp juncea Red fescue

NOTE: This is only a general list of seed that you will find available – there are of course, many more that may be available as plants – see opposite page for addresses.

SUPPLIERS

SEED AND PLANT
SUPPLIERS
Ashton Wold Wildflowers
Ashton Wold
Nr Peterborough PE8 5LZ
Tel 01832 73575

Emorsgate Seeds
Limes Farm
Tilney All Saints
King's Lynn
Norfolk PE34 4RT
01553 829028
(specifies county of origin)

British Wild Flower Plants
Burlingham Gardens
31 Main Road
North Burlingham
Norfolk NR13 4TA
01603 716615
www.wildflowers.co.uk
(specifies county of origin)

HV Horticulture Ltd
Really Wild Flowers
Spring Mead
Bedchester
Shaftesbury
Dorset SP7 0JU
01747 811778

Suffolk Herbs
Monk's Farm
Coggeshall Road
Kelvedon
Colchester
Essex CO5 9PG

Landlife
The Old Police Station
Lark Lane
Liverpool
L17 8UU

Kingsfield (tree nursery)
Broadenham Lane
Winsham
Chard
Somerset

FOR FRESH, VIABLE
YELLOW RATTLE SEED
Sticky Wicket
Buckland Newton
Dorchester
Dorset
DT2 7BY
01300 345476
EMAIL:
stickywicket.garden@virgin.net

FOR DAY COURSES IN
WILDFLOWER GARDENING
Address as above or see
www.stickywicketgarden.co.uk

OTHER USEFUL
ADDRESSES
Flora Locale's website (only)
www.naturebureau.co.uk

Butterfly Conservation
PO Box 222
Dedham
Colchester
Essex CO7 6EY
01206 322342

Flora-For-Fauna
c/o The Natural History
Museum,
Cromwell Road
South Kensington
London SW7 5BD
020 7942 5000
www.nhm.ac.uk/science/
projects/fff/

Flora and Fauna International
Great Eastern House
Tennyson Road
Cambridge CB1 2DT

The Wildflower Society
68 Outwoods Road
Loughborough
Leicestershire LE11 3LY

Plantlife
21 Elizabeth Street
London SW1W 9RP
020 7808 0110

Royal Society for the
Protection of Birds
The Lodge
Sandy
Bedfordshire SG19 2DL
01767 680551

The British Trust for Ornithology
The Nunnery
Thetford
Norfolk P24 2PU
01842 750050

The Wildlife Trusts
The Kiln
Waterside
Mather Road
Newark NG24 1WT
01636 677711

Friends of the Earth
26-28 Underwood Street
London N1 7JQ
020 7490 1555

INDEX

ACKNOWLEDGEMENTS

For their unparalleled inspiration I am eternally grateful to: Clive Farrell who, by his great example and kindness, inspired and led me to become a dedicated meadow maker, and for introducing me to Dame Miriam Rothschild, who first fired my passion for grassland conservation; to Lorely and Mike Brimson for leading me to beautiful, grassy places where wildlife abound.

For their support, both in meadow making and with this book, I am endlessly indebted to: Fizz Lewis, fellow meadow maker and conservationist, for her noble assistance, boundless energy and unfailing encouragement, and both to Fizz and her sons, Rupert and Ben, for dragging me, struggling and whimpering, into the computer age; to Alison Martin, who has strongly supported me through this project and has tried to explain the function of punctuation; to my team of fellow hands-on meadow makers – especially my husband, Peter, and my brother-in-law, Marcus – Northamptonshire farmers, born and bred to the land, bringing old experience and traditional skills as well as new energy to the Sticky Wicket projects; to Shane Seaman, who works so sensitively and helps us with the conservation of local plants; and to Susan Berry, Steve Wooster, Ed Brooks and Anne Wilson for helping to make this book everything I hoped it would be.

My eternal gratitude to Angela Enthoven for allowing Peter and me the opportunity to make many acres of glorious meadows at Hapsford House and to Darren and Ken Lacey, who work with us.

And my special love to Emma Munday, Mark Smith and Lillian White, who help hold just about everything in my life together.